Engaging Our Theological Diversity

Engaging Our Theological Diversity

A Report by the Commission on Appraisal
Unitarian Universalist Association

May 2005

Printed in the United States.

ISBN 1-55896-497-5
978-1-55896-497-6

10 9 8 7 6 5 4 3 2 1
09 08 07 06 05

Contents

Preface

According to the Bylaws of the Unitarian Universalist Association, the Commission on Appraisal is charged to "review any function or activity of the Association which in its judgment will benefit from an independent review and report its conclusions to a regular General Assembly." In 2002 the Commissioners created a mission statement that was inspired by this charge to guide our work:

> Grounded in the living tradition of our free faith, yet charged with acting independently, the Commission on Appraisal's mission is to provoke deep reflection, energizing and revitalizing Unitarian Universalism.

This report is the culmination of four years of labor. It is the eleventh report published by the Commission since it was created with the formation of the UUA in 1961. As its last report, *Belonging: The Meaning of Membership* (2001), was in the final stages of production, the Commission solicited suggestions for its next study and met with many individuals and groups representing different constituencies within the UUA. The ideas and proposals given in this report represent the contributions of a wide range of UU constituencies and individuals, whose wisdom we have attempted to integrate.

First and foremost, we must thank the hundreds of individual Unitarian Universalists who have attended our hearings, participated in our focus groups, completed our surveys, and in some cases gone out of their way to communicate with us in person, in writing, or by email. While their names may not appear in this document (with rare exception, our policy was to use names only for quotes from published or otherwise publicly retrievable sources), we hope they feel that their voices are reflected in its pages.

The cooperation of a number of UU congregations was an invaluable part of our process. By hosting hearings and sharing with us the details of their congregational worship life, they helped us to gain a greater insight into how the issues relevant to this study play out in a congregational context. We are also indebted to the officials of a number of UUA affiliate groups, who helped us coordinate meetings with representatives of their membership: Continental UU Young Adult Network, Covenant of UU Pagans, Diverse and Revolutionary UU Multicultural Ministry, HUUmanists, Process Theology Network, UU Buddhist Fellowship, UU Christian Fellowship, UUs for Jewish Awareness, and the Ohio-Meadville District Youth-Adult Committee. The members of the General Assembly Planning Committee, the UUA General Assembly Office, the UUA Youth Office, and the officers and staff of the Central Midwest District facilitated some of the organization of these meetings.

A number of ministers shared with us sermons inspired by or relating to the theme of this study. Several ministerial study groups also took up our topic and shared with us the products of their collegial process.

Several UU scholars, theology school faculty members, and UUA staff members also met with us. We met individually with Rev. Dr. George Kimmich Beach, Rev. Dr. Thandeka (Meadville-Lombard Theological School), Judith Frediani (UUA Faith Development Office), Revs. Pat Hoertdoerfer and Dave Petee (UUA Family Matters Task Force), and Rev. Dr. Rebecca Parker (president, Starr King School for the Ministry).

Our editor, Mary Benard, and the staff of the UUA Publications Office played an integral role in helping to convert almost four years of thought into one reasonably coherent volume. Mary's patience and fortitude were of absolute necessity in working with the hydra that is the Commission.

This report is a corporate document, created through a collegial process among the Commissioners. We appreciate the contributions of former Commission members Janis Eliot (Portland, Oregon), Charles Redd (Fort Wayne, Indiana), and Rev. Roberta Finkelstein (Sterling, Virginia). Their term of service included the first two years of this study, during which the topic was selected and refined and the methodology of the study was planned. Some of the sections of this report were based on drafts written by them.

We appreciate the efforts of UUA president William Sinkford, who is an ex officio member of the Commission, and of General Assembly moderators Diane Olson and Gini Courter.

The Commission invites comments on this report and on other matters of concern to the Association. Written comments or inquiries may be addressed to the Commission on Appraisal, c/o Unitarian Universalist Association, 25 Beacon Street, Boston, MA 02108. We can be contacted electronically through our website at www.uua.org/coa, or by email at coa@uua.org.

Rev. Orlanda Brugnola, Brooklyn, New York

Dr. James Casebolt, St. Clairsville, Ohio

Joyce T. Gilbert, Rochester, New York

Mark Hamilton, Toronto, Ontario

Rev. Dr. Earl K. Holt III, Boston, Massachusetts

Rev. Dr. Linda Weaver Horton, West Vancouver, British Columbia

Janice Marie Johnson, New York, New York

Manish Mishra, Washington, DC

Rev. Dr. Tom Owen-Towle, San Diego, California

Framing the Question: What Holds Us Together?

The Unitarian Universalist Association is a family of congregations, each of which is a family of individuals. The corporate story of the UUA, therefore, is a product of the weaving together of the stories of individual Unitarian Universalists. During the course of this study, the members of the Commission spent a great deal of time listening to the stories UUs have to tell about diversity and unity: their experiences, their feelings, and their aspirations. We would like to begin by sharing some of the ideas and stories that many UUs have shared with us over the last four years:

> It's the First Principle in living flesh. It's the care and respect and compassion that we all have for each other, it's the support network for all of these people who may not get that hammock of caring and of love that they need, they might not get it at home or at school, and it's here for them, unconditionally. I think that's what really makes it work and holds [the district youth community] together. —*a youth focus group participant*

> I have a vision of the UU movement as interreligious dialogue. As we respectfully share those things of ultimate importance to us we are mutually transformed. This is a model for the rest of the world, a better way to do religion. I believe that we do not need *theological* unity in our theological diversity. —*two adult GA workshop participants*

Unitarian Universalist congregations are often congregations of people who didn't fit in. And so we create communities that are awkward, because that's how we know how to be!

To me this is where the UUA falls down, and why you have CUUPS and the Buddhists and the Christians and all these little subgroups— because we offer the hope of a spiritual journey, and we offer no tools to do it with. We stay in the head, and we don't talk to the heart . . . . [What people need] is touching and tasting and smelling and being, and not just talking about touching and tasting and smelling and being. —*two adult focus group participants*

I wish that there were more of a focus on [conversations about theology and beliefs] because I've been personally really struggling with it, and I sometimes get really scared about death and God and where am I going to go, because I'm scared to death that there's nothing, and honestly I'd rather believe in God and heaven and die believing I'm going somewhere than just dying and saying, "I'm going nowhere." Sometimes I really wish I were Christian just so that I'm not scared at night. —*a youth focus group participant*

[UU Christians] understand exactly what [the humanists] feel, because their sense that "I am in the process of being thrown out of the house that I built," that's where we were—we understand that completely. . . . The question is to somehow change the system so that . . . it doesn't hold that possibility anymore. . . . We tell the story of the increasing tolerance always, but we don't say, "And people lost their church."

Having a common belief would actually allow for more diversity. We talk about class issues and race issues, all those things, the need to have something to hold us together, and we don't have a belief that does, so it ends up being class, or it ends up being race, or it ends up being educational level or economic level. And that's a problem. So I think having a common belief would allow us to become more diverse in all those other ways.

I'm no longer convinced that you can have the omni-inclusive church, you can have the one-size-fits-all church, or even the one-size-fits-all denomination. But I think that's kind of the cultural common wisdom that goes around the UUA, that is what we're trying to do. And I think that's part of the pain of talking about trying to find a center, because we're all so terribly worried that we're going to find a center that excludes somebody. —*several adult focus group participants*

The world needs the message of our liberal faith. There are so many voices crying out for the UU message of inclusion, democracy, and justice.

One thing has become clear, however. Despite consensus within the church that the liberal message of Unitarian Universalism is important in this troubled world, we find it difficult to articulate that message clearly. Conversations with UUs across the continent lead us to wonder: Is our theological diversity getting in our way? These conversations lead us to believe that our theological diversity is not as much of a problem as UUs' inability to do the hard work of finding common ground to build a strong, effective religious voice. In the words of UU historian Conrad Wright, "Even the freest of free churches needs . . . discipline if it is to last long enough to accomplish anything of value in this world."[1]

Our theological diversity is not as much of a problem as UUs' inability to do the hard work of finding common ground to build a strong, effective religious voice.

This report can be seen as a continuation of the last several Commission on Appraisal reports. The underlying theme running through those studies concerns the nature of the UU community: how we are together. The theme begins with *Interdependence: Renewing Congregational Polity* (1997), which examines the relationship between and among the congregations that gather in voluntary association to form the Unitarian Universalist Association. *Belonging: The Meaning of Membership* (2001) examines the relationship between and among individuals who gather in voluntary association to form our congregations. In this way, we have been moving through concentric circles of organization toward the center—assuming, of course, that there is a center. Thus the current question: What is, indeed, at the center of our faith? What is it that holds us together? To refuse the challenge and the opportunity afforded by the question, "Is there a unity in our theological diversity?" is to back away from one of the most important issues affecting the UU faith today. As Walter Herz writes, "Theological diversity alone is an entirely inadequate basis for a strongly associated congregation of individuals, or for a truly functional association of congregations."[2] Not to take up this question risks being "reduced to an agglomeration of liberal religious boutiques, loosely associated and without any real organizing principle."[3]

The selection of this topic was a complex process that began four years ago with a long and amorphous list of suggestions and recommendations, collected from previous commissioners, individual UU ministers and laypeople, and UUA staff members. Through judicious combining and culling, we came up with a short list of six potential topics. One Commissioner volunteered to serve as an advocate for each topic and write a brief position paper in support of it. After all this effort, the final decision was clear-cut—the proverbial "no-brainer." All the topics had value and would have benefited the UUA and Unitarian Universalism with further study. With the exception of theological diversity, however, we felt that the absence of a study on each of the other topics would not leave the Association in danger—that the UUA would be allowed to continue in an acceptable, but perhaps not optimal, way.

We concluded that an examination of the topic of unity in our theological diversity might even be necessary for our very survival as an association of congregations; we foresaw that the status quo, in the long run, could lead to an insecure future for the UUA, a future in which conflict resulting from theological tension could do irreparable harm and potentially lead to schism or fragmentation. We concluded that a study of this issue, while risky, had the potential to establish a healthy basis for the future development of Unitarian Universalism.

One person who has been thinking in great depth for many years about the issues raised in this report is Gordon McKeeman, a retired parish minister and onetime president of Starr King School for the Ministry. We first saw McKeeman's views articulated in a sermon he delivered in 2002; he expanded on these ideas in a lecture he delivered at the 2004 General Assembly in Long Beach. McKeeman suggested that many of the problems and issues Unitarian Universalists have encountered and struggled with in recent years may actually be symptoms of the underlying problem that was created at the inception of the UUA at consolidation. Faced with the messy possibility that identifying a core for the consolidated movement might be too contentious, we seem to have decided instead to leave a question mark at the center.

Several years ago, then–UUA president John Buehrens talked about the developmental history of the UUA. He suggested that our movement might be ready, as it turned forty, to move from adolescence (which he defined in terms of a tendency toward reactivity, antiauthoritarianism, and lack of self-definition) to greater maturity. Current president William Sinkford has taken up the maturity theme, as evidenced by this quote from his well-publicized "language of reverence" sermon:

> I believe that Unitarian Universalism is growing up. Growing out of a cranky and contentious adolescence into a more confident maturity. A maturity in which we can not only claim our Good News, the values we have found in this free faith, but also begin to offer that Good News to the world outside these beautiful sanctuary walls. There is a new willingness on our part to come in from the margins.[4]

The fact that we have chosen to probe the question of what is at the core of our faith is another sign of that maturity. We as a Commission are those who are called upon, as one former member said on a number of occasions, to "catch the wave and ride it." We can surely say we did not invent this topic, nor create the urgency of addressing it. But we are the ones who have gathered up all the threads of desire and need, and boldly (or foolishly) asked the question out loud and even tried to answer it.

Pluralism is an integral part of our faith. The Principles of the UUA "affirm and promote the inherent worth and dignity of every person."

However, despite a growing diversity in our communities and our congregations, intolerance persists. UU minister and liberation theologian Fredric Muir writes, "As a nation and as a religious movement, there appears the possibility that we will find ourselves on the wrong side of history because we are not prepared for the changes that are taking place."[5]

Today, Unitarian Universalism is predominantly a faith of "come-inners," those who joined the church as adults, with a minority of "born-inners," those who were born or grew up as UUs. We may come from the faith tradition of our childhood, or we may come from no faith tradition at all. Most of us have in common, however, the experience of being raised in a tradition other than Unitarian Universalism. Stories abound of UU congregants saying, "I was always a Unitarian Universalist, but didn't know it," or "I finally found a church community where I could express my beliefs and have them accepted." Gatherings of newcomers express joy at finding a community of like-minded people. At the same time, there are some substantial differences between the "come-inners" and "born-inners" among us, differences that are potential sources of tension and conflict.

Another colloquial name for someone who was raised in the tradition is "*gruu-up*." Sometimes it is paired with the term "*nuubie*" for a come-inner; however, this seems to imply that someone who wasn't raised in the faith is a newcomer, even if he or she has been around for twenty years. Another term that often gets used is "*birthright UU*," which can have connotations of entitlement or superiority. In this report we use "born-inner" and "come-inner," for brevity and the principle of least offense.

It is worth being aware of the tensions that sometimes arise between the two groups. Born-inners often feel like a minority in the denomination (which they are), and that their particular needs are overlooked in catering to the large majority of relative newcomers. Conversely, come-inners sometimes feel that born-inners express an attitude of superiority, for example as expressed in terms like "birthright UU." Inasmuch as this attitude is projected, it is likely at least partly defensive, because of the feeling of being a minority.

In general UU congregations do much better at meeting the needs of relative newcomers than those of longtime members.

We believe there are several good reasons for talking about the differences between born-inners and come-inners. First, born-inners really do have some different needs than relative newcomers, needs which are often shared by longtime members, whether they grew up UU or not. However, in general UU congregations do much better at meeting the needs of relative newcomers than those of longtime members. Second, UUs (especially born-inners) do talk about these differences, and so the conversation is already happening. It is worth being part of it. Third, those who grew up UU have a unique sense of the story and culture of the movement, and a depth of experience of the tradition, that cannot be found elsewhere. They often go into the ministry or other positions of leadership. We are not suggesting in any way that come-inners are less valuable than born-inners, but we feel it is worth taking account of the particular experience of born-inners, and the unique contributions they can make.

The well-being of our movement depends on how we deal with these issues. In spite of all the different growth strategies employed over the years, our membership numbers have barely kept pace with population growth since consolidation. Many mainline denominations are actually declining, in spite of the fact that they have a clearly defined set of beliefs, so the lack of clarity in our movement is not the only factor contributing to our lack of growth. However, the generations coming to maturity today and in the next decades are showing a renewed interest in spirituality, and if we can catch their attention, we can become again a prominent and influential religious movement. It is about catching the wave—the wave of people hungry for a sense of belonging and meaning, people who want a place where they can safely pursue a spiritual path in the company of people who will support and challenge them; a place that embraces reason, yet transcends the rational and touches the soul.

However, the consensus of experts from an array of fields—from organizational development to systematic theology—is that to grow effectively, a religious organization needs clearly defined boundaries. And one cannot put even the most permeable boundary around nothing.

These developments in our movement are happening against a backdrop of war, terrorism, economic insecurity, political polarization, and cultural upheaval. As human beings and people of faith, we are seeking not only ways to speak and act prophetically for justice and peace but a balm for weary souls. As President Sinkford said, "UU minister Walter Royal Jones, who headed the committee largely responsible for their current wording, has wondered aloud how likely it is that many of us would, on our death bed, ask to have the Principles and Purposes read to us for solace and support."[6] The commissioners believe that Unitarian Universalists can do better in the solace and support department, and we believe this study may alleviate some of the longing for comfort so often articulated by those who are not quite satisfied with Unitarian Universalism.

One fact has become clear in the course of our conversations with UUs concerning the issue of theology: With rare exceptions, conversations about beliefs and theology are not regular features of our congregational life. Repeatedly, people have told us, "We don't talk about these sorts of things at my church." Everything we have observed suggests that we commissioners are breaking a taboo that Unitarian Universalism took on subconsciously at consolidation—the taboo against talking through the need to merge theologies. This taboo seems to have been based on a fear that if we start to talk about our beliefs, we may discover we are totally incompatible with one another, and our congregations will fall apart.

At a minimum, there is a rarely articulated fear of giving offense—what

Rebecca Parker of the Starr King School for the Ministry referred to in our meeting with her as a "culture of niceness." We often give lip service to the ways in which theological diversity enriches our congregations—and there is no question that it *could*. However, all the evidence suggests that in fact, growing theological diversity within the UU culture—where tolerance and acceptance are considered paramount values—more commonly makes individuals so afraid of offending one another that conversation about belief and theology is stifled. "Encouragement to spiritual growth" is a stated goal of congregational life in the UUA's Principles, and the rich theological milieu present in most of our congregations would seem to be fertile soil for such growth; but if people are afraid to talk about and experience the diversity before them, then the potential for growth will be stunted.

If people are afraid to talk about and experience the diversity before them, then the potential for growth will be stunted.

Although this report is an outgrowth from previous Commission reports, it was also influenced by the reaction of the larger UU movement to those earlier reports. Many individuals have suggested that these earlier documents, especially the last one, on membership, were timid and did not go far enough—that the Commissioners were holding back or "pulling their punches." We have therefore been encouraged, from many circles, to be bold, resolute, and even provocative this time.

One of the goals of this report is to promote the notion that a healthy diversity requires common ground. The theological differences among UUs, while acknowledged at a superficial level, are not discussed and examined with openness, care, and intentionality in broad UU circles. Our commonalities are more subtle, and they are easily missed, ignored, or forgotten. Our differences can seem huge, even irreconcilable, but through the development of consensus around other issues, we can see those differences as a source of enrichment rather than as a threat. Some of the recommendations in this report will focus on procedures and methodologies for discovering these bonds of shared community.

We hope this report will give people permission to talk about beliefs without fear of harming their congregations. And we hope it will, in some way, offer a model for structuring a conversation about belief that is respectful, civil, and fruitful.

One issue that should be clarified is the place of the Commission on Appraisal within the governance structure of the UUA, specifically its relationship to the elected administration of the Association. The Commission tends to regard itself as a creature of the General Assembly: We are elected by the GA delegates, we are funded by the General Assembly, and we report to it, not to the administration. While the president of the UUA is an ex officio member of the Commission, the individuals who have held the presidency in recent years generally have seen the independence of the Commission as a vital part of its functioning and have been careful to avoid influencing the Commission's work.

With these points in mind, it may also be noted that as the Commission was developing its topic of study, current UUA president William Sinkford was beginning to articulate his goals for the UUA and initiating a conversation in UU circles about a "language of reverence." Thus, Rev. Sinkford's efforts and our report are on parallel but independent paths. While the Commission has met with Rev. Sinkford a few times and has raised the topic of his goals and how he views his impact to date, neither party has attempted to influence the other. Rev. Sinkford was not involved in the writing of this report, was not present when its format or content was debated or drafted, and has not been privy to the many conversations that took place between our face-to-face meetings during the years leading up to the publication of this report. The fact that the president and the Commission came to similar conclusions independently of one another about the issues of vital concern to our movement should serve to highlight their prominence and urgency: We ignore the question of how we talk about and manifest theology in our congregations at our peril.

Methodology

In planning our strategies for collecting information, we made a deliberate effort to combine multiple methodologies that would enable us to explore relevant questions both widely (by getting information from a large number of individuals or congregations) and deeply (by creating situations where people could reflect thoughtfully and deliberately over an extended period, considering the relevant issues from a number of angles). Given our limitations in terms of time, funding, and staff support, it was impossible to accomplish both these goals effectively at the same time. By using several different methodologies, however, we were able to bring together a body of information that we believe possesses both depth and breadth.

We began our process with open hearings held during our quarterly meetings, inviting participants from UU congregations in the area. Such hearings were held in Phoenix, Arizona; New York City; Hingham, Massachusetts; Oregon City, Oregon; and Evanston, Illinois (as part of the Central Midwest District's annual meeting). The number of attendees varied from nine to more than fifty, creating different social atmospheres and opportunities for varying levels of exploration. The questions we asked and the kinds of responses we elicited evolved over the course of the project. While the early hearings were fairly informal and less structured, the later hearings used a methodology in which we asked attendees questions like "What is the center of your personal faith?" and "What is the center of the common faith of your congregation?" We asked them to respond individually and in writing prior to sharing aloud with the group and reflecting on commonalities, differences, and themes.

We held similar hearings at the 2002 Quebec City and 2003 Boston General Assemblies. The procedure we planned for the 2002 GA hearing was similar to that used at the local hearings. However, we dramatically underestimated the degree of interest in our topic: We were counting on attendance by about fifty people and were assigned to a room that only held one hundred. Yet nearly two hundred people came to the hearing. Anticipating a larger turnout the following year, our 2003 GA methodology included opportunities for individual responses as well as small-group discussion, allowing attendees to compare views and be inspired by one another. The 2003 hearing was attended by about 230 people, who spent the last half of the session discussing their individual responses in groups of approximately fifteen, with facilitation from Commissioners.

Another very important aspect of our methodology was focus groups, in which small numbers of people sharing some common characteristic were brought together to respond to a series of questions individually and as a group. We pilot-tested potential questions with focus groups of young adult campus ministry participants in Portland, Oregon, and with congregational members in Kent, Ohio. At the 2003 General Assembly, focus groups were conducted with members of theological identity groups (Covenant of UU Pagans, HUUmanists, Process Theology Network, UU Buddhist Fellowship, UU Christian Fellowship, and UUs for Jewish Awareness). We also held focus groups with young adults and youth at GA as well as with youth attending a conference in the Ohio-Meadville District. These focus groups allowed for deep exploration of issues we believe to be central to our study.

Using a less structured format, we also met with students and faculty from our theological schools. In April 2003, the Commission met with a group of five faculty and staff members and five students at Meadville-Lombard Theological School. In October 2003, we had the opportunity to meet with Starr King School for the Ministry president Rebecca Parker and a few Starr King students during our joint meeting with Collegium, an annual gathering of UU scholars from across the continent.

The ordained members of the Commission invited ministerial study groups to take up the central questions of our study. A few accepted the challenge, and a number of sermons from these ministers and from others who were inspired by hearing about our study or participating in the hearings described above were submitted for our consideration. We also solicited feedback from members of the Humiliati and the Congregation of Abraxas, two religious orders that existed for short periods of time in latter twentieth-century UU history.

Taking advantage of the opportunities available to us at General Assemblies, members of the Commission attended workshops and panels on issues relevant to our study. We shared these resources with one another and in some cases followed up with presenters or participants with questions specific to our deliberations.

At the deepest and most personal level, we interviewed a number of individuals who, because of their experiences or expertise, had unique insights into the issues we were considering. These included UU scholars, theologians, historians, and members of the UUA staff, especially in the area of religious education and faith development.

We also used survey methodology in several ways. Short surveys were used in studying several congregations in different regions of North America as well as with members of the Diverse and Revolutionary UU Multicultural Ministry (DRUUMM). A longer, more complex survey was given to 170 ministers, most of whom were recruited at the professional days held prior to the 2003 General Assembly, as well as to 271 lay members of four disparate congregations.

Our broadest methodology was a survey of congregational worship practices, distributed in December 2003 to every member congregation of the UUA worldwide. This survey was completed and returned by 370 congregations—a response rate of about 35 percent, almost unheard of for mail surveys, for which response rates are generally between 10 and 15 percent. While the majority of participating congregations were American, we also received completed surveys from Canada and abroad. The responses generated by this survey gave us greater insight into the degree to which congregations vary in their level of theological diversity and the degree to which this diversity is expressed in the communal worship experience.

We hope this brief overview of our methodology will engender confidence that the insights, conclusions, and recommendations presented in this report reflect the experiences, feelings, and thoughts of a broad sampling of UUs, not just the twelve Commissioners who served during the period of this study.

Metaphors for Unity

The range of theological views represented in our congregations' collective pews is certainly wider than ever before.

We began our exploration of this issue with a label that may imply an inherent value judgment, *theological fragmentation*. The range of theological views represented in our congregations' collective pews is certainly wider than ever before in the history of our merged association or its precursors; however, some feel that the term *fragmentation* implies that this shift from relative homogeneity to diversity is a bad thing, a view with which some, if not most, UUs would disagree.

The term *theological diversity*, while less obviously value-laden, may in fact have its own, positive, bias. Would it be socially acceptable, in our Association's current culture, to question the inherent value of diversity of any sort?

The struggle we went through to develop a working title is illustrative of the complexity of the issue. We considered, "Is There Unity in Our Theological Diversity?" but this implies there may in fact not be. "Where Is the Unity in Our Theological Diversity?" assumes there is some sort of unity. People may infer from the latter title that we believe unity must be theological, but this is not necessarily true. Our unity may be around values, practices, or even some nonreligious aspect of identity, and not around shared beliefs at all. In other words, while our diversity may be theological, our unity may be something else entirely.

While our diversity may be theological, our unity may be something else entirely.

Over the course of the study, members of the Commission struggled continually with exactly what we have been trying to understand, and our thinking has evolved over time. In the course of conversations among ourselves about the topic, as well as those we have held with others, a seemingly natural tendency to fall into analogy and symbolic thinking arose. This may have been helpful, considering the words of Biblical scholar Marcus Borg:

> Metaphors can be profoundly true, even though they are not literally true. Metaphor is poetry plus, not factuality minus. That is, metaphor is not less than fact, but more. Some things are best expressed in metaphorical language; others can be expressed only in metaphorical language.[7]

Thinking in metaphorical terms about the issue of what holds UUs together may provide a psychological distance that helps us explore options our emotional sensitivities would otherwise prevent.

The initial proposal that led to this study included a quotation from theologian Martin Buber that became a useful point of reference for the Commission. This quote contains its own metaphor:

> The real essence of community is to be found in the fact—manifest or otherwise—that it has a center. The real beginning of a community is when its members have a common relation to the center overriding all other relations; the circle is described by the radii, not by the points along its circumference.[8]

The circle analogy captures some aspects of community that are relevant to the issue of how the range of theologies to which we adhere affects our congregations. The center of a circle is a common reference point for all points on the curve; it is equally important to all the points and equidistant from them. The center can be thought of as a common source, as a bonfire around which a circle of people may gather for sustaining warmth. And of course, a circle can have only one center.

Do we have a common reference point at the Association level? Considered separately, can it be assumed that the members of a congregation have a common reference point? Are there even just a few things, let alone a single thing, that we would all see as equally important and as "overriding all other relations"?

Several variations on the center idea have arisen, each more colorful and suggestive than the last: The handle of the umbrella provides support, something to grab onto, and holds together the parts of the whole. The central post of the schoolyard merry-go-round is the point around which everything revolves, a center in terms of activity. It also keeps the whole thing grounded and cohesive and prevents it from flying apart. The maypole is the common reference point of the shared dance experience.

Is there a common "handle" available to all UUs? What is it that holds us together in spite of our own centrifugal force?

A parallel analogy to the center of a circle is that of a core. In a piece of fruit, growth occurs from the core outward. Viewed historically, Christianity clearly is that from which we have grown. But can a commitment to the humanity of Jesus still be thought of as somehow central for us on an institutional level, or have we collectively moved so far from our origins that its relevance is limited? A living cell has a nucleus at its core; it holds the genes that define the organism. It has been suggested that our current crisis of identity is partly rooted in a failure to merge the unique theological perspectives of our ecclesiastical ancestors in the Unitarian Association and the Universalist Church. Imagine the combining of sperm and ovum without the blending of the genes at the core.

Do we indeed have a core? Or perhaps more appropriately, do we still have a core? Or has the evolution of our community outpaced the evolution of our self-understanding?

Yet another perspective suggests that Buber's emphasis on the center rather than the circumference is backward: a community *can be* defined by its circumference if that edge is seen as a boundary, the way a vessel or a living cell is defined or bounded by its outer surface. As much as UUs wish to be inclusive and welcoming, from a sociological point of view membership in a community or group is based on the sharing of some characteristics that people outside the community tend not to share; distinctiveness requires the making of distinctions. But with the Unitarian Universalist dedication to freedom, UUs are averse to drawing lines and marking boundaries, and this hesitancy has made it difficult for us to define ourselves relative to other faith communities in the larger religious economy. This difficulty with self-definition has in turn sapped our energy for evangelism.

However, defining the boundary of the UU community is not necessarily at odds with the UU commitment to freedom, if we allow individuals to decide for themselves which side of the line they are on. Consider the typical modern interpretation of the inclusion of a "liberty clause" in several statements of belief developed by our Universalist forebears, such as the Winchester Profession of 1803. While commonly thought of as allowing individual Universalists to disagree with corporate affirmations of faith, in fact the intent of a liberty clause was to accommodate some variation in congregational creedal statements within the covenant of the national church.

Does the UU community have a boundary? If not, should it? Are there beliefs that are incompatible with being a UU? Are there behaviors that are antithetical to membership in UU congregations? In light of the tradition of congregational polity, what function would be served by a statement of shared beliefs composed at the level of the Association? Do the Principles and Purposes serve as such a statement?

The heart is another commonly mentioned analogy for what we are trying to identify. A heart is a source of sustaining life, a motivating force, a place from which energy emerges. A heart is necessary but not sufficient for human life; an individual's survival is impossible without it but it isn't good enough by itself. The heart may not be large, but it is vital. The concept of "credo," usually thought of as a statement of individual belief, can be traced etymologically to the notion of "that to which I give my heart"—a commitment that is more emotional than intellectual in nature.

Does our faith have a "heart"? If so, what is it, and is it healthy? If not, how long can the Association live without one?

At one point, the commissioners started to move away from the center symbolism and to conceptualize our primary dilemma as identifying what holds us together as a community. One commissioner suggested the old Protestant hymn, "Blessed Be the Tie That Binds" as a new working title. While offered in jest, this phrase does suggest another useful analogy. Many UUs like to imagine church members as sharing a journey up Gandhi's mountain of truth. Mountain climbers are belayed on their shared journey, all tied to a common rope so they can keep track of each other, safeguard each other, and move together in a coordinated way. The image of some sort of shared tie or common thread seems quite useful in describing a community. A group of people binding themselves together in a covenant is an important image in the burgeoning small-group ministry movement.

What are our common threads? If we have trouble identifying them, is it because they do not exist or just that they are hard to cast in words with which everyone can agree?

All of these analogies are useful. Each brings important and unique questions to the fore. But the range of questions makes clear how vast this issue is and how foolish we would be to think we can address them all to our satisfaction or to yours. And yet these questions are of incredible importance to the continued viability of the Association and the UU movement.

There is one more question to bring up in this introduction. In gathering information for this report we have talked to literally hundreds of people for varying amounts of time. They have shared their views and experiences with us, told us many important things, and given us numerous brilliant ideas. But the most important thing anyone has said to us may have been an off-the-cuff question, not a well-thought-out statement. In our interview with her at the 2003 Collegium, Starr King president Rebecca Parker asked us this: "What features of Unitarian Universalism, if you took them away, would leave us with something that is no longer Unitarian Universalism?"

What features of Unitarian Universalism, if you took them away, would leave us with something that is no longer Unitarian Universalism?

This single question is vast in scope, but if we could agree on even a partial answer it would be incredibly useful to the UU movement. Working on this question may help UUs to define that which is vital and essential to our faith. It suggests Theodore Parker's distinction between the transient and the permanent in Christianity, which inspired the UU Ministers Association to publish *The Transient and Permanent in Liberal Religion* in 1995.[9]

During our workshop at the 2004 General Assembly in Long Beach, California, we asked those in attendance to struggle with this question individually, then to share their answers with a partner, and then with the whole group if they were willing. Creativity and excitement in response to this question were palpable in the room. One of the Commissioners joked that we would "capture the final answer this afternoon." We did not do that, although the ensuing conversation was both provocative and evocative. The engagement the question produced, especially in light of the many, many UUs who have told us how infrequently such conversations arise in their congregational lives, suggests a hunger for exploration of serious issues of theology and institutional definition.

As provocative as it is, Dr. Parker's question leads to one that is even more provocative but also riskier: What, if you *added it*, would make Unitarian Universalism no longer Unitarian Universalism? In other words, in addition to considering what is necessary or essential to Unitarian Universalism, we must also ask what is antithetical or contrary to Unitarian Universalism. In the course of our brainstorming of potential data-gathering questions, one suggestion was, "What would a person have to do, or believe, to get thrown out of a UU church?" The fact that we can even formulate such a question suggests that there are UU antitheticals, just as there are UU fundamentals or quintessentials. To understand Unitarian Universalism thoroughly, we would need to identify both.

What does it mean to be a Unitarian Universalist? Given the theological relativism into which we tend to slide in an attempt to preserve the comfort of our theologically diverse community, why should someone be a UU as opposed to anything else? How can we define what it means to be a UU, both for the benefit of those of us on the "inside" and in order to enhance the understanding of the larger society?

We hope to show that these questions matter, that some have answers, and that others still need answers. The chapters that follow correspond to the broad topics the Commission has identified as current or potential sources of unity amid our theological diversity: history, culture, values, theology, worship, justice making, and community.

Earlier in this introduction, we mentioned that some UUs have reacted with anxiety over this report, and have feared that its final outcome will be some sort of creed. This anxiety may have a linguistic component, specifically a confusion of the terms *unity* and *uniformity*. There is a major difference between the two. A community of people can be relatively uniform in practice or procedure, yet not be unified in purpose or vision. On the other hand, a diverse community can still come together in a bond of unity. ". . . Unity rises above all accidental variations, and embraces all differences that are not in themselves incompatible with unity. Uniformity merely makes people resemble one another; it is being and doing as parts of a whole that gives them unity . . . ."[10] Our goals in this study concern unity, not uniformity: why unity matters, where it currently exists and where it does not, what can be done to enhance it, and what might befall our association if it is lost.

The study topic we selected seemed absolutely vital to the continuing health and well-being of the Association. We hope that both the answers we suggest and the unanswered questions we raise will fulfill the Commission's charge to revitalize Unitarian Universalism.

Notes

1. Conrad Wright, quoted in Walter P. Herz, ed., *Redeeming Time: Endowing Your Church with the Power of Covenant* (Boston: Skinner House, 2001), 41.
2. Herz, *Redeeming Time*, 117.
3. Herz, *Redeeming Time*, 119.
4. William Sinkford (sermon, First Unitarian Church (Second Parish), Worcester, MA, Dec. 1, 2002).
5. Quoted in Herz, *Redeeming Time*, 59.
6. Sinkford, 2002.
7. Marcus Borg, *Reading the Bible Again for the First Time: Taking the Bible Seriously but not Literally* (San Francisco: HarperSanFrancisco, 2001), 41.
8. Martin Buber, *Paths in Utopia* (Syracuse, NY: Syracuse University Press, 1996), 135.
9. Dan O'Neal, Alice Blair Wesley, and James Ishmael Ford, eds., *The Transient and Permanent in Liberal Religion: Reflections from the UUMA Convocation on Ministry* (Boston: Skinner House, 1995).
10. Donald Attwater, quoted in Nikolaus Liesel, *The Eastern Catholic Liturgies: A Study in Words and Pictures* (Westminster, MD: Newman Press, 1960), xi.

History: Where Do We Come From?

UU history, the story of our past, has been suggested as one of the unifying elements of contemporary Unitarian Universalism. It may be that in the absence of a common doctrine or creed, religious beliefs, scripture, *mythos* or cosmic story, or distinctive liturgical tradition (except perhaps the remnant of a vaguely Puritan minimalism), what UUs share is a sense of connection to a common past. Indeed, the celebration of that past, and especially of particular individuals associated with it, is a notable feature of many introductory UU pamphlets, sermons, and newcomer classes (not to mention T-shirts).

Awareness of our historical origins and pride in our past accomplishments is fitting and proper, but progressive movements and liberal institutions often regard their own history with ambivalence. The story of the past we most like to tell is of leaving it behind. The heroes of UU history are those who have been the reformers of tradition, those who questioned or even defied the conventions of their time. Where it is not openly rebellious, the liberal spirit is at least restless. A legendary Universalist minister, when asked what Universalists stood for, famously replied, "We don't stand. We move." In fact, we commonly refer to ourselves not as a church or even a faith but as a movement, implying that what we have been is not what we will be, or even what we are now.

But as the Unitarian theologian Henry Nelson Weiman, among many others, has pointed out, true progress has a conservative as well as a radi-

Progress, distinguished from mere change, retains what is of value from the past even as it rejects what has been proven untrue, unworthy, or not relevant to the present.

cal dimension. Reformation has an element of retention as well as rejection. Progress, distinguished from mere change, retains what is of value from the past even as it rejects what has been proven untrue, unworthy, or not relevant to the present. Harvard president (and Unitarian) Charles W. Eliot declared at the dawn of the so-called "progressive" era in 1886 that, "The world could not spare its adventurers and pioneers; but for one pioneer it needs a thousand conservers, in order that all the good the past has won or the present wins may be held fast and safely transmitted" to the future.[1]

By its nature the church is in this sense a conservative—that is *conserving*—institution. It exists to uphold and preserve through time what it considers worthy and precious values. Here is where the church's ambivalence toward its own past works against the notion of history as a source of unity in contemporary Unitarian Universalism—especially in a wider and largely ahistorical American cultural context. The theme of "leaving the past behind" fundamentally calls into question the positive value of any heritage or tradition, even our own. A tradition exists on the basis of what it maintains or strives to maintain over time, what it affirms rather than what it has seen fit to reject. T. S. Eliot, scion of a distinguished Unitarian family who converted to Anglo-Catholicism at midlife, spoke in 1936 to the limitations of mere rebelliousness and the generic dilemma of liberalism:

> In religion, Liberalism may be characterized as a progressive discarding of elements in historical Christianity which appear superfluous or obsolete, confounded with practices and abuses which are legitimate objects of attack. But as its movement is controlled rather by its origin than by any goal, it loses force after a series of rejections, and with nothing left to destroy is left with nothing to uphold and with nowhere to go.[2]

Even without accepting his despairing prophecy, many would agree with the premise that the energy of liberal religion is primarily centrifugal; it knows what it rejects better than what it affirms.

Two Separate Movements

All of this is complicated by the fact that Unitarian Universalism is the heir of two histories, not one, and though they share certain elements in common, they also differ. The hymn that was sung in Boston's Symphony Hall in 1960 at the conclusion of the service celebrating the consolidation of the two national organizations oversimplifies the matter:

> As tranquil streams that meet and merge
> And flow as one to seek the sea,

Our kindred fellowships unite
To build a church that shall be free.[3]

But where there is real freedom there is little tranquility, as the history of the twin streams of our past aptly demonstrates.

The Unitarian and Universalist movements emerged and evolved separately during the formative years of the American Republic. Universalism, centered on the doctrine of universal salvation, was organized as a separatist church, in a manner similar to that of early Baptists and Quakers. In contrast, what came to be called Unitarianism in America was from its beginnings less focused theologically; it evolved for a long time as a tendency less than as a doctrine, a growing rejection of the Calvinist orthodoxy of the Puritan-Congregational churches of New England, especially in eastern Massachusetts. Though their enemies labeled them Unitarians, a name they eventually accepted, they did not intend to create a separate church; they were united in their opposition to what they called sectarianism, and preferred to think of themselves as simply "liberal Christians." Besides, the name Unitarian didn't really fit. They were more concerned with what classical theology calls the "Doctrine of Man" than the Doctrine of God, and in that sense shared some of the same concerns as the Universalists. Their Enlightenment sensibilities were offended by the Calvinist doctrines of human depravity, original sin, and pre-destination, which held that human beings have no control over their ultimate destiny. The right to self-governance, which inspired the Revolution, was rooted in all these religious ideas, and it is no accident or coincidence that so many of the founders of the Republic were liberal in their religion as well as in their politics.

In contrast to the Universalists, who were united in a church organization, an ecclesia, the American Unitarian Association, created in 1825, was made up of individuals, not churches; it was essentially a clergyman's club. Not until the formation of the General Conference, under the leadership of Henry Whitney Bellows at the end of the Civil War, did the Unitarians organize themselves ecclesiastically, and they never abandoned their fierce devotion to congregational polity, rooted in the precepts of the Cambridge Platform recommended to the churches of New England in 1648. It was this Unitarian polity or ecclesiology that was affirmed in the formation of the UUA.

So, though American Unitarianism and Universalism shared some sources of inspiration and their separate histories intersected at several points along the way, each had its own distinct heritage and traditions. They differed in theology and polity, social biases and cultural emphases, and institutional habits.

The Universalist minister Gordon McKeeman—a notable leader before, during, and after consolidation—has remarked that "the road [to consolidation] was not a smooth highway." There were two main issues, he argued: "One was theological, the other ecclesial. One was about our message, the other about our method." In both, "Unitarians and Universalists had important differences."[4]

The process leading toward consolidation focused minimally on theological differences and primarily on resolving methodological issues. The effort was successful in institutional terms, creating a common structure acceptable to both groups so that consolidation could be achieved. Unitarians and Universalists were thus merged organizationally, but theology was more or less left alone. A former member of the Commission has written:

> We took two religious movements, each with clear and distinct historical roots and at least some clear and distinct theological assumptions (such as the oneness of God, the goodness of God, the universality of salvation) and merged them organizationally without attempting to sort through the theological issues. In fact, we seem to have dealt with the thorny issue of potential theological disharmony by essentially banning all theology from the newly formed movement![5]

Arguably, this is the underlying reason for this report: to address the issues left unresolved at the time of consolidation.

Arguably, this is the underlying reason for this report: to address the issues left unresolved at the time of consolidation.

The common religious root of Unitarianism and Universalism is Christianity, specifically liberal Protestantism—although the relationship of UUs with their Christian roots is more fraught than friendly, less a source of unity than of reactivity and contention. It is worth asking whether consolidated Unitarian Universalism, especially as it has evolved in the last half-century, represents an extension of the historical theology of either Unitarianism or Universalism, or whether it is a denomination that is distinctly different from both its predecessors.

An examination of the events of the 1950s, the period right before consolidation, provides an important historical context within which to understand the current situation in our Association and congregations. Fortunately, we have a ready resource, a kind of snapshot, of the Association at the period of its creation, a report entitled *The Free Church in a Changing World*. This publication has not received as much attention as the formative 1936 Commission of Appraisal report, *Unitarians Face a New Age*, but like that earlier document it provides a fairly comprehensive picture of the state of Unitarian Universalism at a critical point in its history.

Consolidation took place in a period of strong numerical growth in institutional religion in the United States, in particularly for the mainline Protestant and Roman Catholic churches. For American Unitarians it was the best of times. The reported membership grew from about 350 churches and a membership of some 60,000 at the end of the World War II to over 150,000 members in more than 650 active churches and 350 fellowships at the time of consolidation.

The situation for the Universalists was quite different. Unlike the Unitarians, whose religious and especially cultural influence was always disproportionately greater than its small membership would suggest—Unitarians never numbered more than one-tenth of one percent of the American population—Universalism was a populist movement that ranked among the largest six or seven denominational groups in America at its height in the mid-nineteenth century. From that peak, Universalism declined precipitously in the last years of the nineteenth century and continued its downward trend in the first half of the twentieth. Many different explanations have been offered for this decline in numbers and influence, including the following:

At its height Universalism was characterized by doctrinal clarity. While allowing for latitude of individual opinion in matters of theology, it was a church and a movement unified by a fervently held belief in the doctrine (or heresy, as others would call it) of universal salvation—that an infinitely loving and merciful God would ultimately redeem or save all people. In a period when hellfire-and-damnation preaching still gripped the religious imagination of many Americans, the doctrine of universal salvation was not only controversial but also compelling for many people. Agreement on this one crucial doctrine, while allowing for wide-ranging diversity of belief in regard to all others, may have been key to uniting a large and growing body of believers who were otherwise characterized by theological diversity. Whatever the cause, as the formative doctrinal clarity of Universalism diminished, so did the number of its adherents.

Another possible explanation argues simply that "Universalism won." Over time the threat of hellfire lost its appeal; its power to influence the popular imagination was overcome by the general optimism and political progressivism that characterized the latter nineteenth and early twentieth centuries. While conservative evangelical preaching never abandoned the threat of hell, over the course of the twentieth century the mainstream of American Protestantism increasingly came to de-emphasize the wrath of God and the prospect of damnation in favor of the love of God and the promise of paradise. Polls today indicate that many more Americans believe in heaven than in hell.

While never formally abandoning the doctrine of universal salvation, the term universalism gradually acquired a broader meaning, implying the idea of a "universal church" characterized by acceptance of an ever-widening variety of religious beliefs. The poet Edwin Markham penned a quatrain entitled "Outwitted" that was widely quoted by both Unitarians and Universalists in the 1950s:

He drew a circle that shut me out–
Heretic, rebel, a thing to flout.
But Love and I had the wit to win:
We drew a circle that took him in![6]

The irony is that as Universalists attempted to expand their circle of faith, the number of their adherents continued to decline.

As the two denominations accelerated their discussions about consolidating their national organizations during the 1950s, they also manifested a growing ambivalence toward the liberal Christian heritage of both. Among the Unitarians this ambivalence had a long history, traceable as far back as the movement's first great theological controversy, over the source of religious authority, which was associated with Ralph Waldo Emerson, Theodore Parker, and the other Transcendentalists of the mid-nineteenth century. It was even more prominent in what came to be called the Humanist-Theist Controversy—a debate essentially about whether Unitarianism should be God-centered or human-centered that assumed its clearest form during the first half of the twentieth century. (Its echoes can be heard even now.) The Unitarian Christian Fellowship (UCF) was founded in 1944 by those on the theist end of the spectrum who felt the need to defend Unitarianism's roots as a biblical faith.

Virtually the only point of theological contention at the Unitarian-Universalist joint meeting to formulate the statement of Principles for the Bylaws of the nascent association concerned its relationship to its Protestant past. Was it *the* Judeo-Christian heritage, or *our* Judeo-Christian heritage? The change from *our* to *the* was ultimately accepted by the delegates, but the importance attached to the issue, as Unitarian historian David Robinson puts it, "indicated the problems not yet resolved among the Unitarians and Universalists."[7]

Along similar lines, Conrad Wright, a Unitarian Universalist and long-time professor of American religious history at the Harvard Divinity School, reminds UUs that "part of our consensus is, paradoxically, what we have agreed to disagree about." He notes further the existence of

some questions, and not trivial ones only, that recur generation after generation, but which never find resolution. An obvious one . . . is the relationship of Unitarianism to the Christian tradition. . . . Is there a minister in the denomination who has not preached a sermon entitled: "Are Unitarian Universalist Christians?" . . . If the time should come when that question is not longer at issue, the denomination will have changed in a very significant way; and I am sure that I would not be alone in regretting it.[8]

As the two denominations accelerated their discussions about consolidating their national organizations during the 1950s, they also manifested a growing ambivalence toward the liberal Christian heritage of both.

Many would argue that, during the last two decades or so, the movement has in fact changed in ways that make Wright's question no longer an issue.

In 1959, at the urging of Dana McLean Greeley, who would become the first president of the UUA, six commissions were established related to the anticipated consolidation. With members drawn from both denominations, the commissions worked together for over three years to produce the report *The Free Church in a Changing World* in 1963. The report identified six major theological emphases current within the movement at that time: Christian liberalism, deism, mystical religion, religious humanism, naturalistic theism, and existentialism, concluding that "the 'liberal perspective' is characterized by openness to different theological emphases which flourish in dialogue with one another." The report further concluded that "certain valuations have characterized almost all religious liberals throughout our history." These valuations were four in number:

- *This-worldly concerns:* a religion that focuses more on the here-and-now rather than the hereafter, and the development of character rather than abrupt conversions
- *Strong ethical responsibility:* a religion involved in efforts for social change and reform
- *Deep commitment to democracy:* a religion which respects individuality and dissent, concerned with insuring the integrity of all. "The same commitment leads liberals to reject mere toleration in favor of true brotherhood."
- *True community is religiously-based:* a religion that strives to transcend individual differences by an inclusive vision and motivation[9]

Having attempted a summary of the theological vision of religious liberals at the time of the Unitarian Universalist consolidation, we now turn back briefly to the earlier history of each movement, by examining some of the widely held affirmations of belief that punctuate their histories. While both movements made ever more careful allowances to protect liberty of conscience and individual freedom of belief, both produced explicit statements of faith, whether formally adopted by an authorized body of the church (as was the practice of the Universalists) or from a consensus derived by less formal means (more common to the Unitarians). This difference derives primarily from the fact that the Universalists were an organized Church, while the Unitarians resisted organization beyond the informal conferences and councils that characterized their congregational polity.

As early as 1803, the Universalists adopted the Winchester Profession, a creed assembled at a meeting of the New England Convention of Universalists in Winchester, New Hampshire:

Article I. We believe that the Holy Scriptures of the Old and New Testament contain a revelation of the character of God, and of the duty, interest and final destination of mankind.

Article II. We believe that there is one God, whose nature is Love, revealed in one Lord Jesus Christ, by one Holy Spirit of Grace, who will finally restore the whole family of mankind to holiness and happiness.

Article III. We believe that holiness and true happiness are inseparably connected, and that believers ought to be careful to maintain order and practice good works; for these things are good and profitable unto men.

This succinct creed includes clear statements on several key theological issues: The first article is a statement regarding epistemology, the source of religious authority on which beliefs are based (in this case the Bible). The second contains, in a single remarkable sentence, a statement of the nature, place, and purpose of God, Christ, and the Holy Spirit—apparently designed to exclude neither the Unitarian nor the Trinitarian position—as well as an explicit eschatology. The third is a statement regarding human nature and purpose.

Since the Unitarians did not even create an organization capable of formal consideration of any such statement prior to the formation of the National Conference in 1865, their early history contains no comparable creed. However, William Ellery Channing's epochal sermon "Unitarian Christianity" (commonly known as the Baltimore Sermon, after the city where it was preached in 1819) came to be widely regarded as the definitive statement of "classical" American Unitarianism. Channing emphasized belief in "the Unity of God," "the Unity of Christ," and most significantly, "the moral perfection of God," reflected in the moral example of Christ, who "was sent by the Father to effect a moral, or spiritual, deliverance of mankind."[10]

The Baltimore Sermon is also notable for its reminder that, like Universalism, American Unitarianism began as a biblical faith. Channing devotes the whole first section of his sermon to a discussion of the right reading of Scripture. The epistemological challenge issued by Emerson, Parker, and other Transcendentalists to belief in the authority of Scripture shocked the first generation of Unitarians and divided the nascent movement. By the time the National Conference was organized at the end of the Civil War, Unitarianism was already a house divided on the issue of its Christian identity. The rift was finally healed, but not resolved, at the National Conference of 1894, where a new preamble to the organization's constitution was unanimously adopted:

The Conference of Unitarian and other Christian Churches was formed in the year 1865, with the purpose of strengthening the churches and societies which should unite in it for more and better work for the king-

By the time the National Conference was organized at the end of the Civil War, Unitarianism was already a house divided on the issue of its Christian identity.

dom of God. These churches accept the religion of Jesus, holding, in accordance with his teaching, that practical religion is summed up in love to God and love to man. The Conference recognizes the fact that its constituency is Congregational in tradition and polity. Therefore, it declares that nothing in this constitution is to be construed as an authoritative test; and we cordially invite to our working fellowship any who, while differing from us in belief, are in general sympathy with our spirit and our practical aims.[11]

Two other Unitarian expressions of belief deserve mention, both for their historical significance and as potential models for approaching our present task. The first, "The Things Most Commonly Believed Today Among Us," was adopted by the Unitarian Western Conference in 1887 "as a non-binding explanation of its theology."[12]

We believe that to love the good and live the good is the supreme thing in religion:

We hold reason and conscience to be final authorities in matters of religious belief:

We honor the Bible and all inspiring scripture, old or new:

We revere Jesus and all holy souls that have taught men truth and righ-teousness and love, as prophets of religion:

We believe in the growing nobility of Man:

We trust the unfolding Universe as a beautiful, beneficent, unchanging Order; to know this Order is truth; to obey it is right, and liberty, and stronger life:

We believe that good and evil inevitably carry their own recompense, no good thing being failure and no evil thing success; that heaven and hell are states of being; that no evil can befall the good man in either life or death; that all things work together for the victory of Good:

We believe that we ought to join hands and work to make the good things better and the worst good, counting nothing good for self that is not good for all:

We believe that this self-forgetting, loyal life awakes in man the sense of union, here and now, with things eternal, the sense of death-lessness; and this sense is to us an earnest of a life to come:

We worship One-in-All,—that Life whence suns and stars derive their orbits and the soul of man its Ought,—that Light which lighteth every man that cometh into the world, giving us power to become the sons of God,—that Love with whom our souls commune. This One we name—the Eternal God, our Father.[13]

It is worth considering what a statement of this sort coming from Unitarian Universalists today would look like and how it might be drawn up.

A second example of unity in diversity is drawn from part of the original Commission of Appraisal report, produced in 1936 and based on the belief that "it would be of incalculable benefit to the denomination if we could contrive to state in definite and explicit terms both our agreements and our points of tension."[14] The Commission offered the following list purely as an example based on its own polling and research; notably, it was drawn up during the period of the Humanist-Theist Controversy, which threatened to divide the denomination.

Unitarians Agree

1. in affirming the primacy of the free exercise of intelligence in religion, believing that in the long run the safest guide to truth is human intelligence.
2. in affirming the paramount importance for the individual of his own moral convictions and purposes.
3. in affirming that the social implications of religion are indispensable to its vitality and validity, as expressed in terms of concern for social conditions and the struggle to create a just social order.
4. in affirming the importance of the church as the organized expression of religion.
5. in affirming the necessity for worship as a deliberate effort to strengthen the individual's grasp of the highest spiritual values of which he is aware.
6. in affirming the rational nature of the universe.

Unitarians Disagree

1. as to the expediency of using the traditional vocabulary of religion, within a fellowship which includes many who have rejected the ideas commonly associated with such words as *God, prayer, communion, salvation,* and *immortality.*
2. as to the wisdom of maintaining the definitely Christian tradition, and the traditional forms of Christian worship.
3. as to the religious values of a purely naturalistic philosophy.
4. as to the adequacy and competency of man to solve his own problems, both individual and social.
5. as to the advisability of direct action by churches in the field of social and political problems.[15]

What would such a statement look like if an earnest effort to state plainly the areas of Unitarian Universalist points of agreement and disagreement were undertaken today?

A Snapshot of the UUA in 1963

The Free Church in a Changing World (1963) was one of the first documents produced after the 1961 consolidation of the Universalist Church in America (UCA) and the American Unitarian Association (AUA) to address the nature and organization of liberal religion in the latter half of the twentieth century. Dana McLean Greeley, former president of the AUA and subsequently the first president of the UUA, chaired the council that coordinated the work of the six study commissions. Paul N. Carnes, the future third president of the UUA, served as secretary. The study commissions were made up of distinguished ministers, academics, educators, representatives of the world of arts and letters, and nonprofit administrators, among others.

With us, theological quandary is not personal, it is institutional.

A statement early in the *Free Church* report addresses the new association's intentional avoidance of theological issues:

> In most other churches, theological quandary is personal. It is not institutional. With us, on the contrary, theological quandary is not personal, it is institutional. We have set at the heart of our church, not a creed or a statement of faith, but the principle that theological questions shall be kept open. We, therefore, have no creed and can have none.[16]

This group did not address the desirability of having some form of unifying statement that would give a clearer shape to the new religious entity.

The most relevant section of the report for our purposes is entitled, "Theology and the Frontiers of Learning." It defines *theology* as a "critical and creative intellectual attempt to express, clarify, defend, reconstruct a religion," adding that any theology is rooted in a particular historical and cultural context; that is, theology is "grounded in the religious life of the community which it serves."[17] Furthermore, wrote the commissioners, "Religion is related to theology as practice is to theory."[18] They also cautioned, "We should never mistake theology for religion, or assume that the concept of theology can adequately substitute for the breadth and depth of religion."[19]

The commissioners working on the theology section gave considerable attention to the importance of truth as a central concern of religious liberalism. They cited Unitarian and Universalist history as "resounding with phrases like 'discipleship to advancing truth,' 'the authority of truth known or to be known,' and 'the universal truths taught by the great prophets and teachers of humanity in every age and tradition'"; then they asked, "Can we ever, however, define 'Truth'?"[20] Noting the importance of truth to science, the writers of this section said, "Probably all members of the Commission would agree that experience is the beginning and end of all science as well as religion."[21]

The 1963 Commission also observed,

Our theology, far from being mature in any evolutionary or historical sense, is in fact in its early stages. Actually we are doing something that seldom if ever has been done before. We are attempting to live out our destiny as a democratic religion. We have set for ourselves the high task of achieving by illumination and discipline the power to transcend frustration, confusion, and Lotus-eater temptation. Thus far we have come to agreement on such general theological affirmations as the humanity of Jesus, individual freedom of belief, congregational polity, and the human origins of the Bible.[22]

"Theology and the Frontiers of Learning" concluded with five specific recommendations:

1. Preserve denominational breadth: avoid identification with any partisanship such as Liberal Christianity, Naturalistic Humanism, and the like.
2. Intensify our dialogue with ecumenical Christianity: inasmuch as our historic roots are in the Judeo-Christian tradition, we should welcome the theological vitality that is returning to that tradition as exemplified in the World Council of Churches.
3. Intensify the dialogue among historic religions: The International Association for Liberal Christianity and Religious Freedom (IARF) can become a workable platform for liberal interfaith dialogue on the relevance of the frontiers of learning.
4. Develop an institute for advanced study of theology in relation to the frontiers of learning: perhaps a university or seminary-affiliated institute to permit intensive and constructive dialogue among theologians, ministers, scientists, and other scholars.
5. Enrich the frontier-content of denominational curricula: this for all ages.[23]

In his commentary at the end of the report, Paul Carnes observed that the 1936 report *Unitarians Face a New Age* "concluded by seeing an important but limited role for the avowedly liberal churches. Today, such conservatism is not warranted."[24] He continued,

Only two things can limit us: lack of support in the churches and fellowships for the movement as a whole, and superficiality. The first can be corrected merely by taking a more responsible attitude toward the Denomination. The second can be met in part by an adequate reception of these reports. We believe that Unitarians and Universalists will not take these as final reports—for there never can be a final report—but will see them as but the conception of a new and vital religious liberalism.[25]

In this chapter we have attempted to demonstrate that the beliefs and practices of our contemporary faith are rooted in UU theological history. The tendency within current American Unitarian Universalism is to express that theological legacy in ethical, non–Judeo-Christian terms. This is worth doing insofar as the Unitarian Universalist faith has continued to emphasize deeds (ethics) and has truly broadened the religious understanding of its members beyond the confines of their Judeo-Christian roots (Unitarian Universalism is genuinely universalistic in this regard).

However, the world's great religions use narrative and metaphor to link theology, ethics, and practice. Modern-day UU religious expression lacks a clear articulation of how Unitarian Universalist narrative, metaphor, theology, ethics, and practice relate to one another. We teach our history (narrative) without explicitly naming the theology embedded within it; we teach our ethics without saying how our theology supports it. It is therefore unsurprising that many UUs have turned outward to find the linkages not yet fully developed within Unitarian Universalism, finding such narrative and metaphor in Christianity, Judaism, Hinduism, Buddhism, Native American spirituality, and other traditions.

Part of the task before us is to strengthen UU institutional identity; we must claim our own heritage, define it as a sacred story, and articulate it as theology, ethics, and practice. This work is under way, and we believe that as it deepens we will find our movement strengthened as we begin to draw more deeply on the theological and spiritual core that already exists.

Modern-day UU religious expression lacks a clear articulation of how Unitarian Universalist narrative, metaphor, theology, ethics, and practice relate to one another.

Notes

1. Charles W. Eliot, address at King's Chapel, Boston, Dec. 15, 1886, in *King's Chapel's 200th Anniversary* (Boston: Little, Brown, 1887), 111.
2. T. S. Eliot, "The Idea of a Christian Society," in *Christianity and Culture* (New York: Harcourt, Brace, Jovanovich, 1968), 12-13.
3. Marion Franklin Hamm, "As Tranquil Streams" (Hymn 145), *Singing the Living Tradition* (Boston: Unitarian Universalist Association, 1993).
4. Gordon McKeeman, "Looking Back, Moving Forward" (president's lecture, UUA General Assembly, Long Beach, CA, June 27, 2004). Also available online at www.sksm.edu/info/journal_images/mckeeman1.pdf.
5. Roberta Finkelstein, internal Commission paper, March 2003.
6. Edwin Markham is often claimed as a Universalist.
7. David Robinson, *Unitarians and Universalists* (Westport, CT: Greenwood, 1985), 174.

8. Conrad Wright, *Walking Together* (Boston: Skinner House, 1989), 33-34.

9. Unitarian Universalist Association, *Free Church in a Changing World* (Boston: UUA, 1963), 25-27.

10. William Ellery Channing, reprinted in Conrad Wright, *Three Prophets of Religious Liberalism* (Boston: Beacon Press, 1954), 74.

11. Quoted in Robinson, *Unitarians and Universalists*, 122.

12. Robinson, *Unitarians and Universalists*, 121.

13. Quoted in Robinson, *Unitarians and Universalists*, 121.

14. Commission of Appraisal, *Unitarians Face a New Age* (Boston: American Unitarian Association, 1936), 32.

15. Commission of Appraisal, *Unitarians Face a New Age*, 33.

16. UUA, *Free Church*, 4-5.

17. UUA, *Free Church*, 23.

18. UUA, *Free Church*, 24.

19. UUA, *Free Church*, 26.

20. UUA, *Free Church*, 26-27.

21. UUA, *Free Church*, 30.

22. UUA, *Free Church*, 34.

23. UUA, *Free Church*, 45-46.

24. Paul Carnes, quoted in UUA, *Free Church*, 157.

25. Carnes, quoted in UUA, *Free Church*, 169.

Culture: Who Are We?

Slightly more than a century ago, the painter Paul Gauguin asked three simple but very profound questions: "Where do we come from?" "What are we?" "Where are we going?" These questions reflect some of the fundamental issues raised in this report. More specific questions are "Where do Unitarian Universalist congregations come from?" and "Why do they exist?" Presumably the answer is that these entities have met and continue to meet the religious needs of an identifiable group of people in ways that no other religious institution can. Why do *individual* congregations exist? Because enough people in a particular geographical area share commonalities in their search for life meaning and choose to band together. What specific needs do they meet for their members, and in what distinctive ways? Here, answers become much more difficult to determine.

Most Unitarian Universalist churches have fewer than five hundred members, and a significant number have fewer than one hundred. Meanwhile, the current culture in the United States suggests that bigger is better: "Megachurches," most of which are founded upon a moderate to conservative Protestant theology, are highly successful in many parts of the country. In many ways they replicate small towns, complete with food courts, art galleries, exercise equipment, and pop-music groups, but they are located in urban and suburban areas, providing a comfortable size of community with a commonality of religious perspective and a worship style that is similar to the general cultural milieu and reflects the television experience with which many baby boomers and generation-Xers have grown up.

In his 2004 book *The Almost Church*, Michael Durrall contends that megachurches attract a younger population that expects leaders to lead.[1] Membership in these churches is easy to the extent that most decisions are made by the paid leadership, who, in turn, expect congregants to follow in clearly defined ways. Some megachurches have denominational affiliations; many do not. Members of these churches often give their religious identity as being part of the specific church, not necessarily as part of a national or international denomination.

What are the implications of this kind of successful church operation, with essentially local congregational polity, for Unitarian Universalist congregations? Several religious organizations have long espoused congregational polity, so this is not a distinctive characteristic. For at least the past forty years, UUs have sometimes described themselves as "differently religious," using the term of religious educator Dorothy Spoerl, but without making clear what the difference is and how it manifests itself. Too often descriptions have been couched in terms of what UUs are *not*—a somewhat antagonistic approach that has been neither satisfying in the long term nor helpful in the short term.

> *It is critical that the Unitarian Universalist Association and congregations within the UUA know their identity. That identity cannot be a club, a social-action organization, or a surrogate family.*

Questions of identity relate to both individuals and societies. It is critical that the Unitarian Universalist Association and congregations within the UUA know their identity. That identity cannot be, as some members suggest, a club, a social-action organization, or a surrogate family, although these functions may serve the needs of individual members at various times. There must be more.

The experience of the Universalists in the nineteenth century explains why: In the mid-1800s Universalists were one of the fastest-growing denominations in the United States. Their distinctive message of the final harmony of all souls with God and of God as love was widely appealing, especially along the Eastern seaboard and in the Midwest. It distinguished them. When this message gained currency in the general population, however, Universalism lost its radical edge, its uniqueness, and it was drawn into a more general Protestant culture, at which point the denomination's numbers began to dwindle.

What is the radical message of contemporary Unitarian Universalism? On what is it based, in what ways does it differ from the message of other organizations (especially religious ones), and how is it promulgated? The UUA leadership talks about "our message" and the need for it, but until and unless it can be stated in a clear, generally understood manner, using language that communicates beyond the UUA's borders as well as within them, that message will not be heard. The current political ethos in the United States is not particularly welcoming to the liberal values that many Unitarian Universalists repeatedly claimed as part of their worldview in the data gathered for this report. This offers both danger and remarkable opportunity, but we cannot seize the opportunity without a coherent message.

For the past several decades, much attention has been paid to the ways in which Unitarian Universalists are different, both from one another and from the wider society. Robert Bellah, a sociologist of religion and an Episcopalian, addressed the latter kind of difference when he reminded listeners at the 1998 UUA General Assembly that the United States is a country with a long history of dissent, historically composed of many immigrants who came here seeking freedom from political and religious oppression in their native lands. Unitarian Universalists tend to be strong dissenters, and therefore, said Bellah, are more a part of the mainstream in this culture than they might like to think. He also pointed out that the first and seventh Principles of the Unitarian Universalist Association are in the reverse order from what is common in most other religious groups: The first refers to every individual, while the seventh, a late addition, refers to the interdependent web of all existence. Furthermore, in his 1985 book *Habits of the Heart*, Bellah contends that an overweening individualism may be anathema to a sense of community of any sort, sacred or secular.[2] This confounds the view that many people expressed to Commission members that a major reason they belong to a Unitarian Universalist congregation is a longing for community.

But this leaves the issue of internal dissent, particularly in theological perspective. When the Commission on Appraisal met in focus groups with theologically oriented organizations within the UUA, numerous participants from most groups expressed a sense of marginalization within the UUA. What, therefore, do people believe to be the current theological mainstream within Unitarian Universalism? No consensus was apparent.

An overweening individualism may be anathema to a sense of community of any sort, sacred or secular.

Data collected by the UUA in the late 1990s and early 2000s through the Congregational Survey used by congregations in search of new ministerial leadership show "eclectic" as the most commonly selected congregational theology descriptor, across the range of congregational size and using a check list of fifteen terms. Congregational members who identify very closely with one or another theological perspective appear likely to feel marginalized—but marginalized by the majority eclecticism rather than by proponents of another theological position. (At the same time, conflict between individuals holding strong and opposing theological views can sometimes occur in a particular setting. Observation and informal research by Commission members has confirmed that significant topics with the potential to create conflict are often avoided within congregations, in the name of harmony but to the detriment of religious depth.)

Time after time, congregations participating in the Congregational Survey said that their congregation has no dominant theology as traditionally defined. One respondent echoed many others when he wrote, "Like many other UU churches, ours has experienced an increase in interest in spiritual practices and worship. Therefore, it was valuable for us to discover that the majority of our members hold traditional UU beliefs." The reporter from another congregation described these traditional beliefs as "humanism and agnosticism," and said members tend to "approach religious questions intellectually or ethically."

Anecdotal evidence from conversations with some current and recent theological school students is suggestive of increasing theistic self-identification among ministers-in-formation. At the same time, recent data from congregations in search of new ministers reveal that congregations most commonly describe themselves as eclectic, with humanism remaining prominent. These observations raise the possibility that, in the future, there may be an increasing disparity between the theological views of UU ministers and of the congregations looking to call them. These theological differences may complicate the ministerial search process and the success of minister-congregation relations.

These changes, as well as others described in this report, merit attention by decision makers. Change is inevitable, though not neutral: It has direction, velocity, and impact. At this time in the life of Unitarian Universalism, intentionality regarding change is critical.

Demographic Reflections

The 1990 National Survey of Religious Identification (NSRI), published in 1994 by sociologists Barry A. Kosmin and Seymour P. Lachman in the book *One Nation Under God: Religion in Contemporary American Society*, offers a picture of U.S. religious affiliations at that time, with analysis. The study, sponsored by the Graduate Center of the City University of New York, was based on a commercial, computer-generated telephone survey of 113,723 people in the continental United States conducted over a thirteen-month period. Widely circulated and discussed at the time it was released, the report showed many more Americans claiming to be Unitarian Universalist than the church had recorded as members.[3] The study profile presented Unitarian Universalists as 0.3 percent of the U.S. adult population as of the 1990 census. The number of respondents self-identifying as UU was 351, yielding an estimated total adult population of 502,000. The reported adult membership at the time (193,411 in 1990) was roughly one-third of this number. Other results from the NSRI study relating to Unitarian Universalists showed them to be more urban and suburban than rural,[4] more likely to be affiliated with the Democratic than the Republican party,[5] and more likely to be female than male.[6]

The report also showed that based on four "Protestant ethic" variables—employment, home ownership, education, and household income—the religious group with the highest average level of socioeconomic attainment was Unitarian Universalists, "a group with a long history of high status in this society."[7] Following UUs in descending order in this category were Christian Church/Disciples of Christ, agnostics, Congregation-alists, Episcopalians, Eastern Orthodox, and Jews.[8] Specific demographic rankings for Unitarian Universalists were as follows:

- Education: 1st (50% college graduates)
- Employment: 11th (53% working full time)
- Income: 2nd (median annual household income of $34,800)
- Property ownership: 10th (73% home ownership)
- Aggregate social status: 1st[9]

While we can't apply this information to the population at large with full confidence, the report is thought-provoking.

In 2001, Barry A. Kosmin, Egon Mayer, and Ariela Keysar conducted a second version of this study, also sponsored by the CUNY Graduate Center, under the title American Religious Identification Survey (ARIS). This time the sample was created by a randomly dialed telephone survey of 50,281 American residential households in the contiguous United States, collected by ICR/International Communications Research Corp.[10] Of the sample, 162 respondents (or possibly 142—both numbers are given by Kosmin) identified themselves as Unitarian Universalist. This number would multiply out to an estimate of 629,000 self-identified UUs in the entire U.S. population. By comparison, UUA membership numbers for 2001, as revised in January 2004, were 218,404.

According to the ARIS study, "only half the UU 'newcomers' also reported membership. Why people say they have switched into but don't belong to their new group is puzzling compared to most 'converts' in other religious groups who are more 'enthusiastic' or perhaps more 'institutionalized.'"[11]

Writing about the 2001 study in the December 24, 2001, issue of *USA Today*, Cathy Lynn Grossman and Anthony DeBarros noted that "two streams diverging from the channels of traditional faith—the trends to solo spirituality and church-shopping consumerism," as reported in the 1990 study, had become "rivers." Grossman and DeBarros also observed the following:

- "Unbelief is rocketing, up from 8% in 1990 to 14% saying they have no religion or they are atheist, agnostic, humanist, or secular."
- The majority of parents in interfaith marriages say they will raise their

children in one parent's faith, "but 13% say they will raise their children with no religion or as atheists, and that this "mix-and-match, come-and-go attitude may be the logical outcome of America's sanctification of individualism and personal autonomy."

- "Millions of people are moving either toward religious groups that require a high level of community commitment or, at the opposite pole, toward a personally defined spirituality."[12]

Our Sociological Identity

We are a people in history. We are also a people embedded in place and in society. We cannot understand ourselves without looking at how we have been shaped, and sometimes challenged, by the society around us and by our own internal culture.

Congregations frequently report difficulties in becoming more inclusive—inclusive of people of diverse races and cultures and also of people who are not middle or upper middle class, educated, and moderately comfortable financially. Individuals from diverse backgrounds may decide to join a UU congregation, but often we do not make it easy. At the same time, we ultimately lose perhaps 85 percent of the young people raised in our congregations.

Class and Race

While a sense of disconnection from the past is a sociological marker of middle-class experience in general, it is particularly a characteristic of those who have dislocated themselves religiously as well as economically and educationally.

Professor David Bumbaugh suggests that UUs tend not only to be primarily middle and upper middle class, but also *emergent* middle class in origin. Many people who come to the church grew up in families not as well educated or liberal-thinking as themselves. While a sense of disconnection from the past is a sociological marker of middle-class experience in general, it is particularly a characteristic of those who have dislocated themselves religiously as well as economically and educationally. This was the life experience, for example, of most of the signers of the Humanist Manifesto.[13] It is rarely the experience, however, of children born into UU families. [14]

Another typical attribute of the middle class is an optimistic view of change and transformation. Bumbaugh points out that transformation as a goal of religion is not universal. Where hopeful change does not appear to be possible in this life, comfort and solace and a sense of dependence on God's love may understandably be more central to the faith perspective. As minister and former Canadian Unitarian Council president Mark Morrison-Reed points out, concern for intellectual freedom is a sign of privilege; the economically or politically oppressed often have more pressing concerns.[15] UU minister Bruce Southworth, looking back over the past century, observes, "Liberal theology with its riskiness, its openness, and its tentativeness is not apt to fare well in a time of political crisis."[16]

How is the UU sociological identity changing, and how is it not? Fifty years ago UUs had a primarily white Anglo-Saxon Protestant identity. Today, more middle-aged and younger come-inners grew up Catholic, non-Christian, or unchurched than ever before, and there are folks of a global range of ethnic backgrounds in UU pews. Thus, UUs are no longer so strongly "Anglo-Saxon Protestant"; however, they remain predominantly "white." People of color make up a small minority of UUs, and that is a source of considerable concern to many in the movement.

These sociological issues are addressed elsewhere in the Association, and we will therefore not focus on them here. We should, however, remember to ask questions regarding class and cultural biases when examining UU assumptions about the world. Are UUs really open to welcoming people who see the world differently? Do we merely tolerate diversity, or can we truly celebrate it? Southworth, minister of the Community Church of New York in Manhattan, challenges us to examine ourselves in the following ways:

> Whose interests are being served by your theological method and affirmations? What class, race, gender, or privileged interest group is benefiting?
>
> Liberal religionists are generally at ease in Babylon despite a social activism that . . . distinguishes Unitarian Universalists from all other groups. Although perhaps expressing sympathy for the poor, there is a gradualist approach that borders on being a "preferential option for the status quo." Power is seldom shared, and the positions of privilege held by so many liberals often go unexamined. Fortunately, liberal religion in its openness to the new, its professed concern for prophetic action, and its inquiring spirit does still include some few who care passionately for a new day.[17]

Gender Roles

While a number of societal changes have influenced the shape of our movement over recent decades, the impact of the changing role of women in the past thirty years has been especially dramatic. The *Report of the Committee on Goals* of the UUA in 1967 provides a vignette of a social reality almost unrecognizable today.[18]

In 1968 women made up 2.6 percent of the UU ministry. By 1988 this proportion had grown to 25 percent.[19] In 1999, the percentage of UU ministers who are women crossed the 50-percent mark. This dramatic change over the past 35 years reflects a shift in the Association as a whole. The Women and Religion Resolution of 1977, a significant step along the way, was largely the work of forward-looking UU laywomen, "aimed at bringing a set of values to the center of our religious faith and practice: relationship, equity and justice, inclusiveness, open process, compassion, and focus on family and children."[20] The increasingly public voices of women in UU ranks have significantly shaped both the psychological and the theological profile of the UUA as a movement in ways we are still discovering.

While not as obvious in the public sphere as in the women's movement, a UU sociological profile at the start of the twenty-first century would not be complete without mentioning the impact of the men's movement, which those of our faith have articulated particularly well. The UU Men's Network has done important, groundbreaking work in this area. Later sections will briefly address shifts in the psychological orientation and theological outlook of men as well as women in the church over the past several decades.

Generations

Alexis de Toqueville noted of the United States during his visit in the 1830s that "each generation is a new people."[21] With the expectations of tradition binding in the United States less tightly than in Europe, he found that generational cohorts were freer to break with the expectations of the preceding generation and forge something new with their lives. This appears to have been particularly true of our Unitarian forebears, who redefined themselves in every generation.

The "baby boomer" generation has had the largest impact on the UU movement since consolidation. Sociologist Wade Clark Roof describes the experience of this generation as a quest for meaning in the midst of a materialism they found unfulfilling. He sees clear signs of a willingness to work for a greater good as well as a greater personal authenticity. Traits that he identifies as characteristic of many boomers sound remarkably like those of UUs:

> Religious identity . . . is rooted less in a self-contained doctrinal heritage or inherited family faith than in their own experience. . . . Members of this generation have few inhibitions about multiple associations with vastly different groups. . . . Even more common is the phenomenon of "multilayered spirituality". . . . Increasingly . . . people identify themselves by adding on layers of experiential meaning to older, less relevant religious and denominational labels.[22]

Many UU boomers became part of the consciousness revolution of the 1960s, embracing both its idealism and its excesses. The Liberal Religious

Youth organization's UUA sponsorship was discontinued in the early 1970s as a result of behavior unacceptable to the youth's elders. Yet a sizeable number of our current ministers bonded with our faith as a result of their LRY experiences.

The sociological profile of Unitarian Universalism braids together a cycle of generations. Each generation has been shaped by different events and tends to hold different values and philosophies. Yet generational theory tells us that the interaction of these diverse points of view can in fact act as a glue holding the generations together. In a sense, they need each other; they complete each other. When UUs are truly intergenerational, open to the gifts and insights of both the old and the young, then our beloved communities of faith cohere in their very diversity. This is a vision UUs are struggling to incarnate.

Impact of the Larger Culture

Members of the generation that came of age in the 1930s and 1940s—identified as "institution builders" and presumably also institution maintainers—are now in their seventies and eighties. They are followed by the baby boomers, a generation that identifies with Unitarian Universalism but doesn't necessarily affiliate with a Unitarian Universalist congregation. They reflect the "bowling alone" pattern described by Robert Putnam in his 2000 book of the same title about the twenty-five-year decline of American civil society; they prefer not to make commitments to a group. They are followed by the cohort sometimes called "generation X," a generation that doesn't want to be part of an "old people's church," that is even more mobile than their parents' postwar generation, and that has grown up in a culture dominated by television and computers.

Today's youth and young adults are strongly attracted to the television programs, movies, and video games that are part of their lives. *The Lord of the Rings* trilogy and *The Matrix* series, for example, raise spiritual, ethical, and intellectual issues that young adults discuss in great depth with their contemporaries. Media is a powerful influence on the youngest generations, and what they see and hear affects their worldviews, ethical judgments, and decisions to an exceptional degree. They may spend an hour or two a month in a church or religious education program, but does this participation come close to the influence of media? Young people's concept of God is shaped by friends and by television shows like *Buffy the Vampire Slayer*, *Joan of Arcadia*, and *Touched by an Angel*. This God, these angels, take many forms, but they are a given. Conversations with agnostic parents or grandparents, not unusual within the Unitarian Universalist world, may be unlikely or impossible, even if the adults are willing to initiate such conversa-

Media is a powerful influence on the youngest generations, and what they see and hear affects their worldviews, ethical judgments, and decisions.

tions—unless the adults are informed about what their children are experiencing in various forms of media. In addition, UU young people are increasingly likely to have friends who are Buddhist, Muslim, Sikh, Hindu, even followers of Santeria, as the United States becomes what Diana Eck describes in *A New Religious America* as "the world's most religiously diverse nation."[23]

These realities have significant implications for the operation of churches and other religious institutions. R. Laurence Moore describes in his 1994 book *Selling God*, how religious leaders in America have gone from frowning upon religion in the marketplace to embracing the promotion of religion through a wide range of commercial media, particularly radio and television.[24] These efforts are sustained, well financed, and effective in reaching people wherever they are, at any time of day and night. Unitarian Universalism has yet to develop similarly effective use of modern media capabilities.

As Diana Eck, director of Harvard University's Pluralism Project, an institute devoted to documenting the evolving and diverse nature of America's religious topography, observes,

> Not only is America changing these (relatively new) religions, but these religions are also changing America. This too is an appropriate question for ongoing study. What does this new religious diversity mean for American electoral politics, for the continuing interpretation of church-state issues by the Supreme Court? What does it mean for public education and the controversies of school boards? What will it mean for colleges and universities with an increasingly multireligious student body? What about hospitals and health care programs with an increasingly diverse patient population? While many people are just beginning to become aware of the changing religious landscape, the issues it has begun to raise for the American pluralist experiment are already on the agenda of virtually every public institution.[25]

This reality affects Unitarian Universalists no less than the more established Christian, Jewish, and Muslim communities.

Most of these "new" religious groups have the numbers to establish their own places of worship, as did immigrant groups before them. Assimilation and intermarriage will occur, as they always have. It is critical to be aware of these changes and make plans to adapt to the new reality. Unitarian Universalists must be prepared to be equal partners in conversations about religion with those whose traditions are well defined, whose rituals can be explained and demonstrated, and whose commitment to those traditions and rituals is firm. This will take more seriousness of purpose than the development of thirty-second "elevator speeches," no matter how well crafted these may be.

Unitarian Universalists must be prepared to be equal partners in conversations about religion with those whose traditions are well defined, whose rituals can be explained and demonstrated, and whose commitment to those traditions and rituals is firm.

Both the NSRI (1990) and ARIS (2001) studies suggested that self-identified Unitarian Universalists comprised 0.3 percent of the adult U.S. population at those times, while actual UUA membership figures reflected only a third of this estimate. More recent figures show an essentially stable adult membership but declining church school enrollment. These are matters of concern. It is entirely possible that congregational membership will continue to decline as a percentage of the population with increasing immigration of people from cultures where their religious practices are well established and an important part of adherents' identities. The likelihood of conversion by these new residents to Unitarian Universalism remains to be seen. A possible result is that UU influence on the national religious and cultural dialogue will dwindle.

We have long been proud of the impact made by individual Unitarians and Universalists on the culture of the United States. At this time it is important to pay more attention to the effect of contemporary culture on Unitarian Universalism. Ever since the 1970s, sociologists of religion and other observers have been telling Americans that mainline churches are in decline because they make too few demands on their members, while congregations with a high threshold for participation and membership are booming. This issue was discussed in the 2001 Commission on Appraisal report, *Belonging*. UU congregations strive to serve the needs of their members but often seem reluctant to require commitment. Congregational life is often characterized by a lack of clarity about the undergirding religious values that the congregation proclaims and desires to practice. This behavior is likely to be self-defeating in the not-too-distant future. What we *are* must speak more loudly and clearly than what we *have been*.

In summary, then, the broader culture offers a number of challenges to Unitarian Universalist religious identity and institutional health at this time in its history. How can we bring our vision and values to a generation raised on media images? What can we do to better communicate the value of being religious "in community"? Are there ways to facilitate dialogue across generations? Are we open to liberal-leaning immigrants, those who have come to a new land looking for a less restrictive culture than the one they left behind?

There are churches in the Association where these things are happening—congregations experimenting with the use of media, articulating the power of community to address troubling social trends, forming intentional partnerships across the generations, welcoming the diversity of immigrants from around the world, and creating religious education curricula around *Harry Potter* and *Lord of the Rings*. Is your congregation among them?

Notes

1. Michael Durall, *The Almost Church: Redefining Unitarian Universalism for a New Era* (Tulsa, OK: Jenkins Lloyd Press, 1983), 29.
2. Robert N. Bellah, *Habits of the Heart* (Berkeley: University of California Press, 1985).
3. Barry A. Kosmin and Seymour P. Lachman, *One Nation Under God: Religion in Contemporary American Society* (New York: Three Rivers Press), 2.
4. Kosmin and Lachman, *One Nation Under God*, 109.
5. Kosmin and Lachman, *One Nation Under God*, 204.
6. Kosmin and Lachman, *One Nation Under God*, 211-212.
7. Kosmin and Lachman, *One Nation Under God*, 257.
8. Kosmin and Lachman, *One Nation Under God*, 258-259.
9. Kosmin and Lachman, *One Nation Under God*, 258-262.
10. Barry A. Kosmin and Egon Mayer, *American Religious Identification Survey*, available online at www.gc.cuny.edu/studies/aris_index.htm.
11. Kosmin and Mayer, *American Religious Identification Survey*.
12. Cathy Lynn Grossman and Anthony DeBarros, "Still one nation under God," *USA Today*, Dec. 24, 2001. Also available online at www.usatoday.com/life/2001-12-24-religion.htm#more.
13. See William Schulz, *Making the Manifesto: The Birth of Religious Humanism* (Boston: Skinner House, 2002).
14. David Bumbaugh, paper delivered to the Refugio Ministers study group, November 2003.
15. Mark Morrison-Reed, *Black Pioneers in a White Denomination* (Boston: Skinner House, 1994).
16. Bruce Southworth, *At Home in Creativity: The Naturalistic Theology of Henry Nelson Wieman* (Boston: Skinner House, 1995), 110.
17. Southworth, *At Home in Creativity*, 122.
18. Committee on Goals, *Report of the Committee on Goals* (Boston: UUA, 1967), 32.
19. UUMA CENTER Committee, *Leaping from Our Spheres: The Impact of Women on Unitarian Universalist Ministry* (Boston: UUMA, 1998), 25.
20. Helen Luton Cohen, "The Impact of Women in Ministry on Unitarian Universalism," in *Leaping from Our Spheres: The Impact of Women on Unitarian Universalist Ministry* (Boston: UUMA, 1998), 18.
21. William Strauss and Neil Howe, *Generations: The History of America's Future, 1584-2069* (New York: William Morrow, 1991), 36.
22. Wade Clark Roof, *A Generation of Seekers: The Spiritual Journeys of the Baby Boom Generation* (San Francisco: HarperSanFrancisco, 1994), 201.
23. Diana Eck, *A New Religious America: How a "Christian Country" Has Become the World's Most Religiously Diverse Nation* (San Francisco:

HarperSanFrancisco, 2001).

24. R. Laurence Moore, *Selling God: American Religion in the Marketplace of Culture* (Philadelphia: American Philological Association, 1994).

25. Eck, *A New Religious America*, 22-23.

Values: To What Do We Aspire?

A number of the Commission's survey respondents have suggested that values—or rather, certain values in particular—are what hold Unitarian Universalists together. The values UUs share are rooted in psychological common ground that appears to transcend differences among individuals' various cultures and faiths of origin.

Psychological Profile

In its research, the Commission found few psychological studies of Unitarian Universalists. However, a doctoral dissertation by Brandon Lael Miller[1] is relevant. Miller studied two groups of fifty Unitarian Universalists, one from New England and one from the Midwest, using a comprehensive battery of psychological tests. He also surveyed more than eight hundred UUs at the General Assembly in Cleveland, using an instrument he created to measure the relationships among "openness," mysticism, and creativity.

Miller draws upon the work of others who included UUs as a comparison group. The following are characteristics he found that may shed light on why UUs have chosen this faith tradition.

Openness to Novelty. Miller used a battery of six measures of openness to novelty in diverse areas of life. The UU subjects scored higher than the general public on all six. Persons of such a temperament find it easier to live with ambiguity and are not as likely to yearn for certainties in their religious perspective. They would be more at ease in community with others who see things differently from themselves. Some people, researchers on temperament find, are more likely to respond to change and novelty with fear and caution, while others respond with curiosity and a sense of possibility. Both "nurture" and "nature" contribute to this pattern.

Risk Taking. On a measure of risk-taking, UU groups tested very highly. This suggests that while many people may be discontented with their religion of origin, those who break away to try a different faith may do so because they find change more intriguing than threatening and because they are temperamentally more open to taking this type of risk.

Creativity. This characteristic, found with greater-than-average frequency in Miller's UU subjects, is closely correlated with openness and risk-taking. In a 1976 essay about the future of Unitarian Universalism as a movement, Irving Murray expressed the hope that UUs can be open to creativity:

> Highly creative people tend to have a taste for complexity and novelty; and are more likely than others to take authority with a grain of salt—to see life in shadings of grey rather than in terms of black-and-white contrasts—to reject dogmatism—to show independence of judgment rather than conformity—to be more willing than others to entertain and sometimes to express their own irrational impulses—to place a greater value on humor—to be freer and less rigidly controlled.[2]

Murray suggests that while this summary "may be read as a description of the (idealized) image we have of Unitarian Universalists," we often fall short of living up to it: "A compulsive need to be independent, different, eccentric, novel, can and sometimes does poison the well of liberal creativity."[3]

A compulsive need to be independent, different, eccentric, and novel, can poison the well of liberal creativity.

Intuitives. Miller's subjects fell disproportionately into the Intuitive rather than the Sensing category of the Myers-Briggs Personality Type index, and this finding is supported by several other studies.

Norms in North America put intuitives in the minority, at about 25 percent of the general population. People who lean toward the Intuitive as defined by this instrument "base their perception on the possibilities in situations, patterns, hunches, imagination, reading between the lines, with expectancy for the future."[4] In contrast, people who lean toward sensing, according to Peter Richardson, are oriented to the present and more literal-minded; they value common sense and tend to be "realistic [and] practical, observing facts directly."[5]

Spiritual Types. UU minister Peter Richardson's model of "spiritual types" takes into account a second Myers-Briggs polarity, one that points to our diversity. While most UUs surveyed are intuitives, we are a mix of *Thinking* and *Feeling* styles in the way in which we engage the world.

This *Thinking-Feeling* preference appears to be both gender- and generation-linked. In the general population, studies suggest 39 percent of men and 68 percent of women prefer Feeling modes. In the Commission's small sample of UU lay respondents, 49 percent of men and 70 percent of women identified as Feeling. Two studies of the UU ministry found 41 percent and 60 percent of males preferring Thinking, while about 80 percent of the women in both studies preferred Feeling. In the Commission study, male clergy respondents who knew their Myers-Briggs types differed significantly by generation: 80 percent of those over age sixty, but only 40 percent under sixty, preferred Thinking. Women, by contrast, differed little by generation. This generational shift among men, as well as the increase in women in the UU ministry, has had significant consequences.

As Richardson explains it, "Thinking sorts for honesty and Feeling for harmony. The spiritual quest needs both sorts of direction, a healthy skepticism and doubt that is firm-minded [thinking] and a passionate quest for meaning that appreciates human qualities with warmth [feeling]."[6]

Richardson postulates that the Buddha was an intuitive thinker, and Jesus was an intuitive feeler. The Intuitive Thinking path is characterized by: "(1) organizing principles operating throughout life and nature; (2) truth that can be global, honest, and clear; (3) social justice as the aim and context for our involvement, including opposition to ignorance with education; and (4) clarity as the basis of spiritual enlightenment."[7] In contrast, Richardson describes the Intuitive Feeling path as: "(1) the quest toward authentic, actualized selfhood; (2) mystical harmony; (3) a life attitude of expectancy; (4) the importance of openness to healing . . . ; (5) social idealism; and (6) focus on process in relationships, familial and social."[8] Many of these same characteristics were mentioned by UUs whom we asked to describe the core of their individual faith.

Self Understandings. A Commission on Appraisal survey of 170 ministers, along with over 260 laypersons (in several congregations and study and leadership groups), asked respondents to rate the importance of a number of characteristics to their personal identities. While the lay sample is too small to let us make any definitive statements, those who responded were surprisingly consistent in their replies to the question of how important to their faith these characteristics are. The respondents saw themselves as people who think and who choose; who love, practice compassion, and are interconnected; who experience and who wonder.

Thinking was a strong identity characteristic, especially for lay respondents. About 89 percent of lay folk and 79 percent of ministers considered this characteristic highly important to their identity. While these scores correlate slightly with valuing "reason" and "humanist teachings," and with male gender, this self-understanding cuts across theological preferences and generations. There was a broader consensus about being people who think and who follow the path of "understanding" than there was around the more specific concept of reason or the philosophy of humanism.

Loving was also valued highly. With little variation by congregation, 82 percent of laypersons and 87 percent of ministers assigned high importance to being people who love. More modestly, 73 percent of laity and 78 percent of clergy highly valued being "interconnected." Similarly, compassion was rated highly by 77 percent of lay respondents and 73 percent clergy. Among laity over age sixty, and across all generations of clergy, women considered compassion more important than men did.

As heretics, (from a Greek root meaning "those who choose"), UUs have an identity as people who choose. This identifier was highly important to 80 percent of laity and clergy. UU Wiccan Margot Adler speaks for many UUs: "One of the great tasks is to help promote choices that aid potential, that promote autonomy, freedom, and cooperation, that allow people to feel whole despite doubt, to act fully and freely despite the uncertainty of being alive in this world."[9]

It appears that "wondering" about our world is something we have in common across our differences (about 80 percent for both lay and clergy across all variables). By contrast, experience as a core self-identifier, while consistent among laity across generation, gender, and sample groups, showed a spread between laity and clergy (at 76 percent and 86 percent).

Outsider Syndrome. While it may not be true within the orbit of Boston, it appears that Unitarian Universalists often see themselves as in some way outsiders or misfits. Although they are often part of the mainstream economically and socially, many experience a persistent psychological lack of belonging. David Bumbaugh refers to this tendency in his Refugio paper mentioned earlier, attributing it to the social dislocation many come-inners have experienced, and a perceived need to "earn their place."[10] People arriving in UU congregations may say, "I have felt like an alien all my life— I thought something was wrong with me because I did not experience the world like those around me did." Even those who grew up in the UU tradition may be subject to this sense of distance from the wider culture. Many experience a degree of prejudice from peers as children because of their religious identity and denial of conventional religious ideas. If, as research on psychological type suggests, nearly 90 percent of UUs prefer a different pattern of perception from the majority of people in the larger culture, this may contribute to a sense of not quite belonging. In his study,

Unitarian Universalists often see themselves as outsiders or misfits.

Brandon Miller makes a considerable point of how people's realities can be substantially different as a result of such factors.

A recent Beacon Press book, *Common Fire: Leading Lives of Commitment in a Complex World*, finds that the common thread in the lives of the one hundred world-changing people interviewed is the experience of marginality—either their own or that of someone they were close to in their young years. This marginality can be either "vulnerability based" (given by circumstances) or "value-based" (chosen).[11] The authors assert,

> Even when it carries a price, marginality can also bear certain gifts: greater self-knowledge, greater awareness of others, and a kind of comfort with life at the edge. The central gift of marginality, however, is its power to promote both empathy with the other and a critical perspective on one's own tribe. . . . Marginality makes it possible to hold several different perspectives and so gain a more complex and sensitive way of seeing, unavailable to those with only one point of view. Held thus in a network of interconnected perspectives—including how one is seen by others—one can develop a deeper, more critical and informed understanding both of the other and of one's own self and tribe.[12]

While UUs' religious marginality may be "chosen," it often allows us to be more authentic about those "given" aspects of ourselves that may not fit in. At our best, any sense of being outsiders can make us sensitive to those who are marginalized by society in more vulnerable and painful ways than UUs are, without the power to make a difference. It gives us the potential to be bridge-builders within our congregations and the larger society, even while we may yearn on some level to be at the center of our own religious tribe. When we hear people saying they feel marginalized in their congregations, UUs might recognize this as a point of both anguish and opportunity.

Stages of Faith Development. Reflections upon psychological profile and faith would be incomplete without considering research on the subject of faith development. These studies are built upon the foundational work of Jean Piaget in cognitive development and Lawrence Kohlberg[13] and Carol Gilligan[14] in moral development. James Fowler first formalized a set of "stages of faith development" parallel to these, and other research has followed.[15] Briefly, Fowler's six stages are seen as developmental through the life cycle. A small child begins with an unformed chaotic world view, stage one, moving in early childhood to one structured by outside authority, stage two. In stage three, "conventional faith," the community defines the individual's worldview. Individuation and independence mark stage four, while stage five is interdependent and open to integrating wisdom from many sources. Stage six points to rare people like Jesus and the Buddha.

Fowler's model (and it is only a theoretical model) must not be seen hierarchically, lest people discount faith qualities such as profound love that may give depth even to earlier stages of faith. Nor must UUs forget that, for people who have known only chaos in their growing years, the imposed order of a stage-two faith may bring hope into their lives.

If we envision a series of concentric circles into which human awareness can expand when the environment requires it, perhaps we can understand why people in a village culture (other than shamans) may never need to extend their awareness beyond stage-three or conventional faith. In a diverse and complex world, however, theoretically higher stages provide people with the tools to encompass more of the reality they experience.

Philosopher Ken Wilbur suggests that the Enlightenment was possible because, for the first time in Western history, a critical mass of people were able to function at Piaget's *formal operations stage* of abstract reasoning, which shows up in complex cultures (if at all) in the early teen years.[16] A recent study found that 43 percent of midlife adults still functioned in the "concrete operations" stage typically developed by children around the age of eight.[17] Harvard studies suggest that only 5 to 10 percent of adults take the step from the dichotomizing reason of Fowler's individuative-reflective or stage-four faith to the dialectical form of reasoning associated with stage-five faith, and this rarely happens before midlife.

Sharon Parks hypothesizes a stage between Fowlers' third and fourth stages, a transitional stage that spans the gap between a conventionally assumed faith and a critically appropriated faith. She sees this as a time of "promise and vulnerability," since never before and perhaps never again are conditions so favorable for forming a life-transforming vision. It is a time of exploration, of probing, tentative commitment, yet this new inner dependence is fragile.[18]

If UUs live up to our values of openness and acceptance, UU congregations can provide an optimal environment for this fragile exploration by young adults, as well as by others who find themselves in a transitional stage as a result of engaging a new faith tradition. So why are young adults not flocking to our doors? Might it be that UUs are often too quick to dismiss anything short of a solid, abstractly reasoning stage-four identity? And what about UU children, who need concreteness as a part of their developmental process? Is their wisdom discounted because it is not expressed in abstract form? How about born-in UU young adults, who might disprove the common wisdom that stage-five consciousness does not develop before midlife?

There are three dimensions of the journey from stage three (conventional) to stages four and five that are of particular interest in the context of shared UU identity. The first is cognitive: How do UUs understand religious authority, and how do we handle ambiguity, paradox, and polarity as we compose our lives? Stage two is characterized by an uncritical trust in an external authority, and there is little or no tolerance for ambiguity. Dualisms are dealt with by casting them as antagonistic, or by collapsing one side altogether. In stage three, authority is given to the consensus of the community, and differences tend to be cast in "we/they" language. Moving toward stage four, a person begins to understand that he or she must use critical thinking to compose a world among a complex diversity of possibilities. Some people may be tempted to try to force a premature or artificial synthesis on the polarities they encounter.

With the unfolding of stage five, we discover that "mature wisdom is not an escape from, but an engagement with, complexity and mystery. Our response to this form of knowing is not necessarily agreement, but it does arrest our attention and compel our respect. . . . Without abandoning the centered authority of the self and a disciplined fidelity to truth, [there is] a new capacity to hear the truth of another."[19]

This experiential level has a transpersonal dimension, characterized by a felt experience of the unity of all reality. A challenge for Unitarian Universalists is not to confuse this transrational perspective with prerational, conventional faith.

Stage five is also characterized by movement from inner dependence to interdependence and from a self-selected, like-minded community to openness to the other; from class-biased universalism to true mutuality with those other than one's own group or class or culture:

> When the conversation with "otherness" is sustained, when one continues to bump up against those who are different, the inner-dependent self begins to find a more adequate truth in a dialectic with the "other" both within and without. A yearning for community (not just association) with those who are profoundly other than oneself emerges. . . . "Issues of social justice are essentially about who is to be cared for and who neglected, who is to be included in our community of concern and who excluded, whose point of view is to be taken seriously and whose ignored. As faith grows, it challenges all established [assumed and conventional] answers to these questions."[20]

As useful as they might be, one must be wary of using stage theories to impose a single vision of wholeness or maturity on every person without respect to the uniqueness of each personality and life story; the worth of doing so is an Enlightenment fallacy, according to the postmodern perspective.

Yet, as a faith tradition, could we understand ourselves to be in the process of moving from a stage-four to a stage-five faith? We are certainly embracing a certain amount of diversity, finding value in dialogue (witness the explosion of covenant groups), and making efforts to hear one another, to include "the other" in an open community and expand our justice concerns. As Sharon Parks says, "Without abandoning the centered authority of the self and a disciplined fidelity to truth, [are we not reaching for] a new capacity to hear the truth of another?"[21]

Values at the Heart of Our Faith

Over the past two years at GA workshops, hearings, congregations, and leadership and ministers' groups, the Commission has asked nearly eight hundred people to tell us about the core of their faith. In addition to data the Commission has collected, this section draws from a 1976 study of UU values by Robert L'H. Miller, a religious studies professor at Tufts University.

Miller distinguishes between *instrumental* values, those that are means to valued ends, and *terminal* values, or those that are valued ends in themselves.[22] The study, according to Miller,

> identified a distinctive Unitarian Universalist paradigm of values marked by a high ranking of the terminal values (self-respect, wisdom, inner-harmony, mature love, a world of beauty, and an exciting life) and the instrumental values (loving, independent, intellectual, imaginative, and logical) which, taken together, show an orientation towards competence rather than morality and stress personal realization, individual self-fulfillment, and self-actualization.[23]

Miller further comments that "Unitarian Universalists appear to emphasize acceptance of others and a non-judgmental approach to differences between persons which diminish the relevance of forgiveness."[24] In addition, "The homogeneous character of Unitarian Universalists seems to be confirmed regardless of the parameter chosen."[25]

The most frequent responses to the Commission about values at the core of the UU faith are in accord with Miller's findings, and many are reflected in the following covenant:

Love is the doctrine of this Church;

The quest for Truth is its sacrament,
And Service is its prayer.
To dwell together in peace,
To seek knowledge in Freedom,
To serve human need,
To the end that all souls shall grow
Into harmony with the Divine—
Thus do we covenant with each other and with God.[26]

Unitarian Universalists appear to emphasize acceptance of others and a non-judgmental approach to differences between persons which diminish the relevance of forgiveness.

The Commission's questionnaire on worship practices found that recitation of some version of this covenant is widely practiced. Whether or not we see common theological assumptions in these commitments, most of the points in this covenant reflect explicit operational values.

The same can be said of the following doxology, named by 75 percent of those congregations responding to the Commission's Worship Survey who mentioned singing a doxology regularly:

> From all who dwell below the skies,
> Let faith and hope with love arise;
> Let Beauty, Truth and Good be sung
> In every land by every tongue.[27]

UUs ranked loving as an instrumental value and mature love as a terminal value more highly than did respondents from other groups, religious and nonreligious.

These two affirmations between them lift up nearly all the values named in core-of-faith statements.

Relational Values

Words that express caring and connection between people, and sometimes beyond the human community, occurred frequently in core-of-faith statements.

Love. A solid 41 to 50 percent of lay respondents and 55 percent of ministers included in their personal core definition one or more of the words *love, compassion, connection,* or *community.* Taken together as variations of the same basic concept, this is by far the strongest value expressed. While different groups emphasized different aspects in this cluster of relational words, being connected in a caring relationship was at the core of faith for around half of the respondents.

Robert Miller's study found that UUs ranked loving as an instrumental value and mature love as a terminal value more highly than did respondents from other groups, religious and nonreligious. Perhaps the UU way of being in community religiously does take a different shape because of the other values we bring to it—and because of those we do not (for example, many faith groups rated such qualities as obedience and self-control much more highly than did UUs).

Community is of particular interest in the above cluster of values. Minister Richard Speck argues that "it is the force of community that holds us together and thus is our center around which all else revolves."[28] Charles Howe, a historian of Unitarian Universalism, disagrees: "My reading of our history is that this [community] has been a major emphasis for only the past forty or so years; moreover, it is an emphasis that is by no means uniquely our own, but shared with those of many denominations."[29]

The Commission found evidence that the importance of community to UUs is growing. The statement "Process in community is core to my spiritual path. Creative engagement in community stretches, deepens, and transforms us" was rated as highly important by 67 percent of lay respondents and 82 percent of clergy, especially women. "As we respectfully share those things of ultimate importance to us, we are mutually transformed," says a GA participant. "This is a model for the rest of the world, a better way to do religion." One minister focuses on "a ministry of mutual hospitality where strangers (*hospes* in Latin) can come together to create relationship."

The information we have collected, especially from large hearings held at the 2002 and 2003 General Assemblies, makes clear that people differ substantially in terms of why they believe community matters in UU congregations. Many people emphasized the instrumental value of community. They wrote about the benefits they gained from being part of a UU congregation and/or the larger UU community—benefits like caring and support, access to resources for exploration and growth, feelings of safety and security, cooperation in social action, being surrounded by like-minded people, and a sense of connectedness. To some, however, community is a terminal value; being in community has an intrinsic value that is not directly related to concrete benefits gained from it. People who feel this way acknowledge that people enjoy important side benefits from being in community, but they express a sense that community itself has value exceeding any practical benefits that accrue from it.

Speck concludes, "Community, covenant, caring are the watchwords for my understanding of what is at the center of our faith. We come together in voluntary commitment to each other to live out our lives with the highest values we can mutually discover. And we pledge to each other our energies to reshape the world for the greater good."[30]

Service. Among the respondents who described the center of their faith, between 16 and 24 percent in various lay groups and 23 percent of ministers mentioned service or a commitment to justice. The several congregations studied varied in their degree of focus on social action. More than one respondent mentioned the Hebrew phrase *tikkun olam*, "to heal and repair the world." Minister Richard Gilbert, author of a UU curriculum on ethics, says succinctly, "To be is to be for others."[31]

Lay respondents speak of their desire to "make this world a better place." "At the center of my faith," says one, is "a quest for meaningful ways to be of service and to enhance the lives of myself and others." For many, service is not only a choice, but a need or call. A GA participant explains, "The need to drive for justice-making lies at the core of my theology . . . the belief that we—humans, not God—are responsible for making and sustaining a just world."

On the Commission's theology questionnaire, 92 percent of ministers and 78 percent of lay respondents rated as highly important the statement "Love and service are core; we respond to the gift of life with gratitude, generosity, and compassionate action." For the UU participants of the 1976 values survey, love and responsibility were third and fourth highest among instrumental values.

Diversity. This has been a growing UU emphasis in recent years, though the word was rarely used in earlier surveys. Broadmindedness, a related earlier value, rated second only to honesty as an instrumental value among UUs in 1976. The minister John Dietrich proclaimed this to be a core characteristic of the religious liberal in a sermon appearing in *The Humanist Pulpit* early in the last century.[32] *Tolerance* is another related traditional word.

In the Commission's study, a deep acceptance of "all who dwell below the skies" was not mentioned consistently as a part of individuals' faith cores. Yet valuing acceptance jumped dramatically when respondents were asked about the core of their *congregation's* faith.

One minister echoed a number of others in speaking of "striving to balance acceptance with transformation; working to open my heart to greater love and compassion and humility." A few respondents specifically mentioned "acceptance and encouragement of diversity and uniqueness."

A UU proponent of liberation theology asserts, "Diversity means embracing otherness and, in so doing, becoming whole. The social distinctions of race, age, class, sexual orientation and gender are easily used as distractions and barriers to prevent community. . . . Diversity offers the gift of wholeness."[33]

The Commission also found positive statements about enjoyment and richness of diversity in packets from congregations in search of new ministers during recent years. A number of search committees mentioned diversity as a positive value: "By design we encourage that all have a place at the table." Another committee wrote, "We are proud that our congregation is racially and religiously diverse." Nor is the diversity limited to that between people: "We embrace a rich mixture of theological orientations, complex both within individuals and throughout the congregation."

Diversity means embracing otherness and, in so doing, becoming whole.

The Search for Meaning

It has been said that Unitarian Universalists would rather seek than find—that they value the journey more than the destination. While this picture may be somewhat exaggerated, core-of-faith respondents underlined the importance of the fourth Principle, commitment to a "free and responsible search for truth and meaning."

The Quest. A cluster of words denoting *quest, transformation, search, growth,* and *learning* garnered a place in "core of my faith" statements from a consistent 25 to 30 percent of respondents in various groups. Valuing growth and learning is congruent with the psychological characteristics of openness, risk-taking, and creativity that surfaced in the Brandon Miller dissertation discussed earlier, as well as with a Myers-Briggs intuitive personality that tends to prefer the realm of possibility to that which already exists. The 1976 values study found that UUs valued "an exciting life" as a terminal value and being "imaginative" as an instrumental value more than did people from other sample populations; UUs gave an even higher rating to "a sense of accomplishment," at sixth among terminal values.

A participant in the Commission's 2003 GA workshop put it this way: "I see Unitarian Universalism as a process or a set of rules about procedure for personal spiritual inquiry. I often call it a discipline—a way of thinking through questions—but not the answers!" Another wrote, "I believe that the path of faith is a path of learning and changing and growing. All else flows from that." A minister described her faith core as "openness to growing, awareness of how I am related to all things, and willingness to be transformed." And a lay woman said that the core of her faith is "exploration—willingness to be open, reshape beliefs, and respect others'."

Valuing "the quest" is a venerable part of our history, going back at least as far as Francis David, who left the Catholic priesthood to become first a Lutheran minister, then a Calvinist, then a Unitarian. The story goes that he told his children that if they ever discovered a more excellent faith, they should by all means follow it. UUs have at times been accused of being forward-looking to the point of abandoning our past tradition.

Charles Howe offers this assessment: "The true core is that strong, free, vibrant intellectual center, that center of free theological intellectual activity, that center always demanding response in the world: that center always in process, always moving ahead through time, leaving its imperfect products in its wake, products that we, by entering that center, are challenged to improve."[34] We, the children of heresy, are still challenged to be "those who choose"—who find the courage to be in new ways demanded by our lives and our times.

Truth. What is the object of our quest? From 15 to 30 percent of various respondent groups offered words such as *truth, understanding, wisdom,* and *curiosity.* "Discipleship to advancing truth" has been a core affirmation throughout our history.[35] It would seem that many among us hold the conviction that "the truth shall make you free," yet what kind of truth has this power? On a Commission theology questionnaire, 76 percent of lay respondents and 63 percent of ministers rated this statement as highly important: "Understanding is core. Study, reflection, reason and observation help us transform ourselves and our world." Among both lay respondents and ministers, this path of understanding was correlated with age.

Also relevant to the question of truth is the nearly unanimous positive response to the statement "We know our truths are partial and our understanding could be wrong: we are open to evolving new insight." One GA participant explains that at the core of his faith is the "humility to viscerally understand that my positions may be wrong. I can hold a position passionately knowing that it is ultimately tentative. Chaos is OK and can even be comfortable."

"Due to the limits of human knowing, it is always incomplete," writes minister Mike Young, a UU pantheist with a Buddhist practice. He continues,

> The community most likely to keep us alive and growing is not one in which we all agree; but rather one that tolerates, affirms, even cherishes the broadest, richest diversity. Not because there is no final truth, but because there may be and our own incompleteness suggests we may not have it yet. . . . And even someone who is quite wrong may have something to teach me.[36]

The 1976 survey of values found that UU respondents assigned more importance than other groups to both intellect and logic as instrumental values. They also ranked wisdom second only to self-respect as a terminal value.

Freedom. Despite the much-emphasized place of freedom in UUs' self-descriptions, this value showed little importance or consistency as core to faith in diverse groups of individual respondents, perhaps because it is considered a given. When asked to describe their congregation's core, however, those who attended Commission hearings in 2002 and 2003 mentioned this value cluster twice as often as they did in describing their own core values. When asked what holds UUs together as a tradition, freedom also shows up more strongly.

"Asking a lot of questions" was central for a number of respondents, as was "freedom in community." Minister Peter Raible looked for a similar balance in finding at the core "individual religious authority bounded in community." One GA participant described the center of faith as the freedom "to draw from the truths of all religions to make meaning in life, and to do this search in a supportive community where we share each other's humanity." Another wrote, "Freedom is the core and not just a starting point. Freedom to keep growing and changing and still be included." Independent thinking was mentioned by others in a more individual context: "The core of my faith is free thinking—creating my own spirituality."

Theology questionnaire respondents overwhelmingly supported the

One GA participant explains that at the core of his faith is the "humility to viscerally understand that my positions may be wrong."

statement "Freedom of conscience and choice are central." While an instrumental value for most, *freedom* (like *community*) appears to be a terminal value for some respondents. Participants in the 1976 values survey rated freedom third among terminal values. Since then, the emphasis appears to have shifted to freedom in community rather than freedom as autonomy.

Our religious ancestors held firmly to the value of freedom while stating clearly that what they valued was not simply "freedom from" but "freedom for." Frederick May Eliot, in a radio talk in 1939 when he was president of the AUA, explained that freedom is

> no mere absence of fetters. . . . There is nothing static about it. Rather, it is by its very nature active, involving a hard and continuous discipline, always outreaching its power . . . enlarging the operations of the mind and the inner life of the soul. . . . If anyone supposes that the Unitarian faith in freedom is an easy faith, he shows a complete misunderstanding of the fundamental nature of this universe. Freedom is something that must be won, and preserved, by the most strenuous effort.[37]

Wholeness

The quality of human life is a traditional concern for Unitarian Universalists. A cautiously optimistic understanding of human nature and potential and a vision of moving toward greater wholeness are often cited as characteristic.

Human Worth. Our first Principle garners a modest 10- to 12-percent inclusion rate in individuals' statements concerning what is at the core of their faith; yet other evidence suggests this historical affirmation remains a key value. UU participants in the 1976 values survey rated self-respect as their highest terminal value, clearly higher than for other groups, religious and otherwise.

A lay respondent stated it clearly: "An essential faith in human nature and its potential good is at the center of my personal faith." Several put this in terms of a sense of the "god" within: "My faith centers on an awareness of the "I am" within, and the learning tools that help me to be always aware and connected to it." For a GA participant, "There is an inherent worth in every person, and it is only through community and the sharing of ourselves that that worth and spirit is found/recognized/given meaning/developed."

Goodness. Between 14 and 20 percent of participants in the Commission's diverse respondent groups used the terms *good*, *responsible*, and *ethical* to describe the core of their faith. A lay respondent focused on "how to turn what I believe into right action." Others referred to the importance of "walking our talk." Humanist Carol Wintermute wrote, "If I have a faith at all, it would center on human possibility, specifically the potential for human beings to educate each other to do 'good.' Not that we've done it yet, but that we could, is what keeps me in the optimist camp and away from the despair of pure skepticism."[38]

Closely related are values of integrity and courage, mentioned by 7 to 10 percent in respondent groups. One minister wrote of "the felt necessity of growing to be the best person I can be, and of leaving the world in the best shape I can." A lay informant centered his faith in "knowing self; and learning to act from my truth without fearing disapproval." Others also wrote of the importance of "learning not to be afraid," for fear can impede acting with integrity. Several mentioned the integrating function of their faith, finding an "urgent need to unite reason, intuition, passion, and experience fully in freedom and love." Another explained, "At my religious/spiritual core is a strong love of intellectual, cognitive, and emotional honesty and integrity."

Although these values received only modest attention from Commission respondents, the 1976 values survey paints a different picture. Among instrumental values, UU responders (although not unique in valuing it highly) chose honesty as most important.

Inner Harmony. Of the respondents to the Commission's theology questionnaire, nearly 90 percent of laypersons and clergy rated the statement "Interior harmony is central to my religious path" as important, and up to 28 percent of individuals in diverse respondent groups mentioned this quality as core to their faith. In the 1976 values survey, inner harmony was a higher terminal value for UUs (fifth) than for other groups.

One lay respondent, describing the center of her faith, wrote, "I need to find that place in myself that is calm, peaceful, and intuitive." Another sought "to live with insight and harmony and for the greatest benefit to my human and natural environment." Other respondents mentioned mystical experience or connection with the transcendent or the natural world. One congregation included a significant number of respondents with a Buddhist meditation practice.

Looking Beyond Ourselves

The nature of connection beyond human community and the relationship of that connection to individual and collective faith are places of both common ground and tension in the contemporary UU movement. Other data would suggest that a sense of being part of an interconnected web appears to be one of the strongest points of consensus, while finding "God" at the core of faith is more controversial. Yet both appeared with similar frequency in core of faith statements.

Beauty and the Natural World. Appreciation of beauty and the natural world as arenas of human experience was mentioned by between 14 and 30 percent of individuals in varied groups. The Miller values survey found that UU respondents rated a world of beauty as a terminal value more highly than did other groups of respondents, well ahead of pleasure and a comfortable life.

A number of core-of-faith respondents mentioned "faith in the interconnectedness and interdependence of all life." Others wrote of valuing the natural world, where they have experienced "a sense of the holy contained within the ordinary." Some appreciate nature aesthetically; others through a sense of wonder at the insights of "new science." Another looks to the Earth: "To see the image of the big blue marble floating on nothing, for me, is to understand the way of peace, to a uniting spirituality for all of Earth's inhabitants." Still others look to the world of human artistic creation as a source of spiritual inspiration.

The Transcendentalists of the nineteenth century had a major role in bringing appreciation of nature into our tradition. Henry David Thoreau, who was raised Unitarian but distanced himself from any formal affiliations as an adult, wrote in his journal,

> I go forth to see the sun set. . . . I witness a beauty in the form or coloring of the clouds which addresses itself to my imagination. . . . You tell me it is a mass of vapor which absorbs all other rays and reflects the red, but that is nothing to the purpose, for this red vision excites me, stirs my blood, makes my thoughts flow . . . and you have not touched the secret of that influence. If there is not something mystical in your explanation, something unexplainable to the understanding, some elements of mystery, it is quite insufficient.[39]

Harmony with the Divine. About 30 percent of ministers and from 16 to 33 percent of respondents in diverse lay groups used language referring to the holy, divine, or transcendent in their core-of-faith statements. One respondent found the center of faith in "the deep-set belief in a great good that lures us forward to our best selves, a.k.a. God." Another speaks of her "deepening experience of and relationship to the Holy, shared in community and encouraged through mindfulness."

Data gathered by the Commission about the core of faith for individuals and their congregations found strong support from Robert Miller's 1976 values study, as well as the writings of past and present Unitarians,

Universalists, and UUs. While many of these values are shared by other religious traditions, our current data support the Miller study's findings of a distinct and widespread cluster of values common to Unitarian Universalists. Our contemporary data also suggest, however, a modest shift in emphasis away from individualistic values in the direction of community.

Caring congregants valuing love and community; curious folk seeking growth, learning, and transformation; committed disciples of advancing truth who cherish wisdom, intellect, and logic; concerned individuals balancing freedom and choice with service to others and a vision of justice; courageous risk-takers pledged to integrity and honesty; creative appreciators of inner harmony and a world of beauty; covenanted people honoring the interdependent web and affirming human worth; compassionate companions who accept one another and respect themselves; and open-minded people learning from dialogue in diversity—Unitarian Universalists aspire to be all these and more. These aspirations, rooted in UUs' own experience, in their dialogue with one another, and in their history as a people and undergirded by an implicit theological world view—these aspirations describe UUs' common ground as a religious people.

Notes

1. This unpublished dissertation was completed at Oxford University in England, where Dr. Miller is now a faculty member. This research was the subject of a presentation at the 2003 UUA General Assembly.
2. Irving Murray, ed., *Highroad to Advance: Charting the Unitarian Universalist Future* (Pacific Grove, CA: Boxwood Press, 1976), vii.
3. Murray, *High Road to Advance*, ix.
4. Peter Richardson, *Four Spiritualities: Expressions of Self, Expressions of Spirit* (Palo Alto, CA: Davies-Black, 1996), 6.
5. Helen Luton Cohen, "The Impact of Women in Ministry on Unitarian Universalism," 27; Commission on Appraisal survey, 2003-2004.
6. Richardson, *Four Spiritualities*, 8.
7. Richardson, *Four Spiritualities*, 45.
8. Richardson, *Four Spiritualities*, 146.
9. Margot Adler, *Heretic's Heart: A Journey Through Spirit and Revolution* (Boston: Beacon Press, 1997), 288-289.
10. David Bumbaugh, paper delivered to the Refugio Ministers study group, November 2003.
11. Laurent Daloz, Cheryl Keen, James Keen, and Sharon Parks, *Common Fire: Leading Lives of Commitment in a Complex World* (Boston: Beacon Press, 1996).
12. Daloz et al., *Common Fire*, 76.

13. Lawrence Kohlberg, *The Philosophy of Moral Development* (San Francisco: Harper and Row, 1981).

14. Carol Gilligan, *In a Different Voice: Psychological Theory and Women's Development* (Cambridge, MA: Harvard, 1982).

15. James Fowler, *Stages of Faith: The Psychology of Human Development and the Quest for Meaning* (San Francisco: HarperSanFrancisco, 1995).

16. Ken Wilbur, *Sex, Ecology, Spirituality: The Spirit of Evolution* (Boston: Shambhala, 2000).

17. Mary Wilcox, "Response to the Tentative Hypotheses Paper from the Moral Development Perspective," in Kenneth Stokes, ed., *Faith Development in the Adult Life Cycle* (New York: W. H. Sadler, 1983), 129.

18. Sharon Parks, *The Critical Years: The Young Adult Search for a Faith to Live By* (San Francisco: Harper & Row, 1986).

19. Parks, *The Critical Years*, 51.

20. Ronald Marstin, quoted in Parks, *The Critical Years*, 68.

21. Parks, *The Critical Years*, 51.

22. Robert Miller, "Religious Value System of Unitarian Universalists," *Review of Religious Research*, vol. 17, no. 3 (1976): 189-208.

23. Miller, "Religious Value System," 189.

24. Miller, "Religious Value System," 194.

25. Miller, "Religious Value System," 207.

26. Covenant by L. Griswold Williams, *Singing the Living Tradition*, reading 471.

27. Composite based on Isaac Watts, *Singing the Living Tradition*, hymn 381.

28. Richard Speck, "The Enduring Center of Unitarian Universalism," in *Unitarian Universalism: Selected Essays* (Boston: UU Ministers Association, 1997), 57.

29. Charles Howe, "The Core of Unitarian Universalism," in *Unitarian Universalism: Selected Essays*, 94.

30. Speck, "The Enduring Center," 60.

31. Richard Gilbert, questionnaire response collected at 2003 General Assembly.

32. John Dietrich, *What If the World Went Humanist? Ten Sermons* (Yellow Springs, OH: Fellowship of Religious Humanists, 1989), 8.

33. Fredric J. Muir, "Unitarian Universalist Diversity and the New Transcendentalism," in *Unitarian Universalism: Selected Essays*, 50.

34. Howe, "The Core of Unitarian Universalism," 96-97.

35. From the "Unitarian Working Principles" document adopted by the American Unitarian Association Board, 1944.

36. Mike Young, "Living with Theological Diversity," in *Unitarian Universalism: Selected Essays*, 34.

37. Frederick May Eliot, *Unitarians Believe* (Boston: American Unitarian Association, reprinted 1958), 21.

38. Carol Wintermute, "Toward a New Synthesis: Gifts of Tradition," in Denise Tracy, ed., *Wellsprings: Sources in Unitarian Universalist Feminism* (Oak Park, IL: Delphi Resources, 1992), 51.

39. Henry David Thoreau, in Perry Miller, ed., *The American Transcendentalists* (Baltimore: Johns Hopkins, 1957), 75.

Theology: How Do We Frame the World?

Do UU commonalities and interconnections find support in common theological ground? Some who have attended Commission on Appraisal hearings and completed questionnaires have doubted this, or even its desirability. Others have offered diverse reflections on how UU values come together into a worldview supported by implicit if not always explicit theological assumptions about the nature of reality.

As we ponder the question of the unifying characteristics of Unitarian Universalism amid its ever-increasing theological diversity, we now explore the religious ideas that continue to define Unitarian Universalism. Areas of understanding historically considered theological include the nature of the cosmos and of human beings, how we know what we know, where we find our religious authority, how we practice our values and strengthen our spirits, what we see as the goal of the religious journey and the nature of religious community, and how we define our mission in the world.

A common fallacy about Unitarian Universalism is that one can be UU and believe anything. In point of fact, the religion UUs understand and practice today emerges from a particular history of ideas. Those ideas, reflecting the tradition's roots, were once clearly expressed in the terms of Western Christian theology. Those earlier explicit expressions of theology have given way to an implicit theology, one that is buried within the seven ethical Principles that the UU movement has officially adopted. Nonetheless, the Principles emerge out of a theological tradition that can be traced back to the most radical, free-thinking branch of the Protestant Reformation. UUs are the product of a particular theology, and our core beliefs continue to implicitly express that theology even as we have shied away from explicitly articulating it.

In this light, it is not accurate to say that UUs can believe anything, particularly in terms of theology. To put forward such a notion cuts the tradition off from its historical and theological roots.

Present-day Unitarian Universalists have a tendency to underemphasize the common theological elements of our faith as rooted in our history. A clearer and more consistent articulation of the theology UUs hold in common, and the origin of these liberal theological beliefs, could be one source of greater denominational cohesion. Religious narrative is a part of every major world religion, and the common theological aspects of the Unitarian Universalist narrative should be named and celebrated.

This chapter is not intended to be an in-depth, exhaustive, or academic study of Unitarian Universalist theology. Rather, we seek to launch a conversation that allows for the fact that Unitarian Universalism *has* an extant theology, a fact frequently de-emphasized in favor of ethics. UU theological roots should be, and are, a source of unity among us, even as UUs find ever more diverse expressions of their liberal theology. We recognize that others are actively working on articulating Unitarian Universalist theology further and more deeply; there is a need and a hope within the movement for this work. We hope that such efforts will deepen the cursory discussion we offer here.

Key Questions

The following discussion incorporates findings from literature review, Commission hearings, GA workshops, and focus groups. It is informed by findings of a brief questionnaire used with three congregations (86 respondents) and a longer theology questionnaire completed by 170 ministers and students (representing about 15 percent of the UU ministry) as well as 279 lay respondents (most of these in four congregations). The statistics quoted below for theological statements are from the second survey. We recognize that conclusions from such a small lay sample can only be suggestive.

What Shapes Our Religious Convictions?

Almost universally among UUs, personal experience is considered the most important source of religious conviction. While support for deriving convictions from one's own experience is consistent across variables, significant gender, generational, and personality-type differences do appear in the comparative importance assigned to reason and intuition. The groups that contrast most strongly in valuing reason as a source of convictions are men over age sixty and women under sixty. Conversely, female respondents value dialogue as a source of conviction more than men do, especially older men.

In UU theologian James Luther Adams's words, "Actuality is richer than thought. There is always a tension between *logos* and being."[1] Past UUA president William Schulz observes that, to his knowledge, with one exception the signers of the first Humanist Manifesto never "talked about religion in terms of *experience*; they talked exclusively in terms of *beliefs*."[2] While recognizing that assumptions do filter experience, UU discourse has shifted significantly over the past eighty years. Humanist Manifesto II, which Schultz signed (along with process philosopher Henry Nelson Wieman), explicitly acknowledged the importance of experience. Is UU faith rooted more in experience than in beliefs? Are UUs fully cognizant of the difference?

Is UU faith rooted more in experience than in beliefs? Are UUs fully cognizant of the difference?

Canadian naturalist David Suzuki states,

> Plato and Aristotle . . . began a powerful process of separating the world-as-abstract-principle from the world-as-experience—dividing mind . . . from body, and human beings from the world they inhabit. . . . The story told by the Western world specifically excludes human experience as a source of truth. We assert an "objective reality," made of abstract universal principles, which is more correct, more accurate than the messy sensory world we experience daily.[3]

Process theologian Bernard Meland puts it this way:

> Experience . . . is not so much an interplay of explicit sensory responses as a bodily event which conveys to the living organism, in a holistic way, its rapport and participation in the nexus of relationships which constitute its existence. . . . Depths and discontinuities harass the inquiring mind."[4]

Where Is Our Religious Authority?

Unitarian Universalists have distinguished themselves from other religious groups by where they look for religious authority. Over five hundred years ago, their forebears challenged the authority of religious institutions. Today, scriptures are seen more often as inspirational than authoritative. Unitarian Universalism's identity as the "free church" has been central to its evolution. So where do UUs today look for religious authority—for what gives legitimacy to their convictions? The italicized statements that follow are items on the theology questionnaire described earlier in this chapter.

"Our primary religious authority is our own experience. Therefore freedom of conscience and choice are central." This assertion is closely related to the above discussion, and almost all of our respondents agree that it is highly important.

UU Wiccan Margot Adler writes, "The battles I would wage would be my own, under my own authority . . . rejecting all answers that did not come from skin and bones and my always ambivalent, continually doubting, heretic's heart."[5]

Biblically centered UU historian David Parke confirms,

> Our concern begins and ends in direct personal experience. While valuing the insights of others, we give highest priority to what we ourselves have seen, heard, touched, tasted, and smelled. . . . While cherishing the testimony of others we demand an original engagement with the world and we are impatient with lifeless truth and borrowed authority.[6]

Postmodern philosophers assert that the very way people experience— what they notice and what they fail to notice, and how they shape their perceptions—is profoundly influenced by their cultures and individual histories. These concerns are at least partially addressed if we understand experience as *encounter* rather than *perception*. Postmodern critiques do affirm that attention to our particularity comes closer to what is real than abstract concepts of a unified reality.

"We deepen our wisdom in community when we share our stories and engage in dialogue across our differences." This affirmation was highly important to 82 percent of lay folk and 91 percent of ministers. The recent popularity of covenant groups attests to a growing appreciation of the power of dialogue as a spiritual practice and recognition of the wisdom to be garnered through challenging yet respectful engagement.

A lay respondent observed that UUs "discern where our hearts are moved in common and grow/connect there. Differences are honored, discussed, and shared, but do not limit our forward motion of spirit." This focus on the power of dialogue in community to help UUs distill truth is not as new as one might think. In her study of the history of covenant in UU tradition, lay theologian and minister Alice Blair Wesley describes our seventeenth-century ancestors as dedicated to doing exactly that. She shows, for example, how church records in Dedham, Massachusetts, describe in detail the house meetings the founders held in 1637 to develop the foundation of their covenant:

Each one could, as they chose, speak to the question, or raise a closely related question and speak to that, or state any objections or doubts concerning what any other had said, "so it were humbly & with a teachable hart, not with any mind of cavilling or contradicting." In other words . . . here we speak our own understandings or doubts. No arguing. The record reports that all their "reasonings" were "very peaceable, loving & tender, much to edification."[7]

"We are committed to the use of reason to interpret our experience and to form and test our religious convictions." A solid 90 percent of those responding to the theology questionnaire considered reason "important." However, a substantially lower number (26 percent of clergy and 46 percent of laypersons) answered "very important." In contrast, 72 percent of the clergy surveyed considered the first Source ("direct experience of mystery") to be "very important," and only 2 percent rated it less than "important."

In the past few years there have been numerous references to the 1995 UU Ministers' Convocation in Little Rock, Arkansas, where some participants were distressed at what they took to be a rejection of reason.[8] Over 95 percent had just agreed to wording to the effect that "a profound experience of the holy" (small h) was at "the core of our faith"; an amendment was proposed to add a phrase about "critical trust in the power of reason" to the sentence. This amendment was defeated, and there was no time to process what that meant and find a resolution. A primary argument of those who voted against the amendment was that reason, as important as it is, belonged logically in the following sentence, as a means of processing and understanding one's experience. Others would agree with Sarah Oelberg's statement in a recent sermon: "I submit that the heart of our faith always has been and still is a devotion to reason."[9] Perhaps the current study can shed some light upon that controversy.

Discovering a "reasonable" faith has been life-changing for some; for others, disciplined inquiry is taken for granted as a way of life.

Among nearly eight hundred respondents to the Commission on Appraisal's query "What is at the *core* of your faith?" only 2 to 4 percent of diverse groups mentioned reason. (When asked about their congregation's center, however, responses were in the 6- to 20-percent range.) Clearly, discovering a "reasonable" faith has been life-changing for some; for others (especially many who grew up UU), disciplined inquiry is taken for granted as a way of life. As for the 10 percent who indicate they do not consider reason important, some agree with minister Richard Erhardt: "When I was growing up I learned that it was all right to say just about anything that was on my mind in my UU congregation. But that right ended if I mentioned the word God."[10] It is a fact of UU history that while some have come to us because their authentic selves were wounded in orthodox Christian (or other) communities, there are also UUs who have had their most precious, life-transforming experiences dismissed by fellow UUs in the name of reason.

Do the Principles and Our History Unite Us?

"Sharing stories from our larger UU faith traditions" garnered a modest 54-percent rating of high importance from lay respondents, while ministers valued it more strongly at 80 percent. UU Principles and Sources, in contrast, were valued similarly by both groups, at just under 70 percent. Though not the case among lay respondents, ministers who grew up in the UU tradition or its precursors found the Principles less important than those who did not. This group valued other aspects of the tradition as a source of convictions somewhat more highly than come-inners did.

A number of respondents did focus upon the Principles as providing a center of faith, for them or for their congregation: "Our center *does* exist: individual search, human dignity, care for world, etc." Some clearly make reflecting upon the Principles a spiritual practice: "I take the Principles *very seriously* and found that the deep reflection needed in life to be faithful to those values has changed me. . . . The different 'Sources' work for different people, for the same *center* (the Principles)."

There does seem to be some confusion about the function of the Principles, however. Some respondents think the Principles "don't go deep enough," or fear they are too often treated as a creed rather than as a covenant among congregations. On the other hand, a GA participant wrote, "I was surprised that in our group we did not say that what holds us together is the seven Principles—that they have to be agreed upon if we stay in Unitarian Universalism."

How Important Are Our UU Sources?

Nothing is more characteristic of Unitarian Universalists than a diversity of self-naming. For example, while 20 percent of the eighty-six respondents from churches surveyed in the New York area chose to call themselves "Unitarian Universalist," over twenty different theological descriptors were mentioned as well. Overall, the Commission's research supports the perception that most Unitarian Universalists draw from diverse Sources, in every conceivable combination.

While 65 percent or more of lay respondents to the longer theology questionnaire consider each UU Source important, no single Source has a clear edge—despite the fact that nearly half of the respondents belong to churches with a strong humanist identity. Gender and generation are significant here: women under age sixty rated the first Source ("direct experience of transcending mystery") significantly higher, and the fifth ("humanist teachings") significantly lower; men over sixty reversed this trend. Comparing these two Sources for mutual exclusion garners a little creative tension: 12 to 16 percent highly valued one while considering the other unimportant. A large majority, however, embraced both these Sources, as well as others.

This is particularly true of the clergy respondents, whose responses showed no significant tension between the first and fifth Sources. The first Source had a clear edge among clergy, as 90 percent rated it highly important. Intriguingly, the greatest contrast here is between male ministers of different types on the Myers-Briggs Personality Inventory: Thinking men valued the first Source least, while feeling men valued it most. Two-thirds of the clergy respondents rated "words and deeds of prophetic women and men" highly important, followed closely by the third and fourth Sources. "Humanist teachings" ranks fifth, with substantial generational and gender variation (nearly all respondents consider these teachings important, but relatively few ranked them as "very important").

Among clergy who completed the theology questionnaire and who briefly described their theological orientation, the language of *process theology* (including panentheism and process naturalism), was used by 32 percent of respondents, the largest proportion. Second was humanism (20 percent). For the most part this is "hyphenated humanism," combined by all but three infor-mants with language related to one or more of the following: mysticism, process theology, God/transcendence, or Christianity. Several also mentioned Buddhism or Paganism. In the 17-to-19-percent range were mystic, Christian, and God/transcendence; Buddhism and religious naturalism are in the 13-to-14-percent range; and pagan and feminist/liberation language clustered in the 5-to-6-percent range. Among the small group of lay respondents who gave descriptors, humanism and process theology each garnered 17 percent. Religious naturalism was third, with 14 percent. Multiple descriptors were common, and over a quarter of the respondents used language outside these categories to describe themselves.

This tendency toward multiple self-naming is showing up in many places in the UU faith. Most search committees in the past several years have adopted survey instruments allowing multiple choices. How people identify themselves theologically depends on many factors, including definitions given and the options offered. The Commission phrased its questions in a way that did not emphasize theological boxes, weighing each Source separately, and also invited open-ended self-naming and core-of-faith statements. It focused upon sources of unity more than points of separation. With the caveat that any conclusions about the perspectives of laity in our movement from the Commission's limited research can only be extremely tentative, the resulting picture is different from that found by two studies in the last decade.

One of these was the "Fulfilling the Promise" survey, completed by about 6 percent of adult membership in 1997. When allowed only one choice and limited options for self-identification, 46 percent of respondents selected "humanist" from the list of options given. Next were earth- or nature-centered (19 percent), theist (13 percent), and Christian (9.5 percent), followed by mystic, Buddhist, Jewish, Hindu, and Muslim in ever smaller percentages. At the same time, when asked what is missing in their UU experience, 52 percent said, "greater intensity of celebration, joy, and spirituality." These results suggest a polarization that may well be somewhat exaggerated by the power of language.

Commissioner James Casebolt[11] conducted another study in the Midwest giving twenty theological labels from which to choose. The results showed respondents "felt the need to circle three or four terms to describe their theological views." About 54 percent selected humanist, 33 percent agnostic, 31 percent earth-centered, 18 percent atheist, 17 percent Buddhist, and 13 percent each for pagan and Christian.

How Do We Understand the Universe?

One of the primary functions of religion is to provide people with a framework for understanding the physical world and their place in it. The Principle that most clearly expresses contemporary Unitarian Universalist cosmology is belief in the interdependent web of all existence. This guiding Principle fuels much of modern-day UU social justice and advocacy work related to environmentalism, animals' rights, economic injustice, and homelessness, among other worthy and related causes.

The current UU understanding of an interdependent and interconnected cosmos has evolved from a theology that we can trace back through our Christian roots to the Old Testament book of Genesis. Genesis is the cornerstone for some of the basic cosmology evident in all three Abrahamic faiths (Judaism, Christianity, and Islam): specifically, Genesis 1:24-31 and 9:1-17. The most common interpretations of Genesis hold that human beings are the pinnacle of all creation. We are God's favored creatures, with everything in creation—all the resources and all the animals—existing for our explicit benefit. Competing liberal interpretations hold that human beings are the custodians of creation, and that our role as custodians invokes great responsibility as well as privilege. Regardless of the interpretation to which one subscribes, both interpretations create a human-centered cosmology—humans are the centerpiece of creation.

These traditional Jewish and Christian understandings of creation were called into question with the scientific revolution and the Enlightenment. With the publication of the discoveries of Isaac Newton in his *Principia Mathematica* in 1687, people began to believe in a "natural law" that governed all aspects of nature and human existence; the challenge for rational thinkers was merely to discover these laws, be they moral or scientific.

The latter half of the nineteenth century saw the development of new scientific understandings that pushed Western thought even further away from the traditional human-centered understanding of the universe. Charles Darwin (brother of a Unitarian minister) published *The Origin of Species* in 1860. Darwin's book helped fuel a decades-long debate on evolutionary theory and the origins of the human species. Our location in an interconnected evolutionary chain implied a cosmology in which humans are merely one piece of creation rather than its centerpiece. Leaders from both the Unitarian and Universalist movements came to be important supporters of Darwinian evolutionary theory and all that it implied.[12]

These legacies from scientific rationalism, the Enlightenment, and Romanticism (which returned mystery and emotion to the equation) led to Unitarian and Universalist views of a universe in which humans are a part of an interconnected, sacred whole. Today, many UUs find expression of this belief through Eastern philosophies (such as Hinduism, Buddhism, and Taoism), Earth-centered traditions, and Native American spiritualities. While the Unitarian Universalist understanding of our place in the universe, our cosmology, is not unique to Unitarian Universalism, it is worth noting that UUs do have a cosmology, and that it stands in contrast to the most common interpretations emerging out of the Abrahamic faiths.

UUs do have a cosmology, and it stands in contrast to the most common interpretations emerging out of the Abrahamic faiths.

This theological evolution was borne out by the Commission's study. Of all the questions asked in the theological survey, "The natural world is a web of interdependent connections, of which we are inescapably a part," is the largest piece of common ground for both ministers and laity. Over 90 percent of respondents, across all demographics, asserted that this understanding is highly important to their faith. The rise of *religious naturalism* as an identifier led to the adoption of the seventh Principle in 1984, and interest has accelerated in the decades since.

One GA participant spoke of "the experience of the presence of life within me, within the present moment, within all people and creatures, and intuition that we all share this life and are intimately interconnected in a fragile and durable network of love." Another wrote, "When we have a *felt* connection to the interdependent web of existence, we trigger a natural inclination to become our best selves. I call the fact of interconnectedness and our inclination to be our best selves God."

UUs' experience of the natural world has led us to acknowledge that we are all profoundly interdependent. The first woman astronomer, Unitarian Maria Mitchell, wrote 150 years ago,

Small as is our whole system compared with the infinitude of creation, brief as is our life compared with the cycles of time, we are so tethered to all by the beautiful dependencies of law, that not only the sparrow's fall is felt to the uttermost bound but the vibrations set in motion by the words that we utter reach through all space and the tremor is felt through all time.[13]

The statement *We do not live in a "two-story" universe where what is "natural" is separate from what is "holy" or "sacred"* is also an area of common ground. Alice Blair Wesley reminds us, "Channing and many other Unitarian teachers of their generation labored all their lives to proclaim: The extraordinary is but the unfolding of what can reasonably be shown by experience to be implicit in the ordinary."[14] UU religious naturalist and professor of religion Jerome Stone writes, "My naturalistic outlook suggests to me that the deeper vision we seek to attain is not of another realm or of invisible spirits, but rather a revised insight into importance of things. There is a 'depth,' not apart from, but right in the midst of things."[15]

What Do We Believe About Sin and Evil?

While present-day Unitarian Universalists continue to debate about what they call *sin* and *evil*, many would agree that, to the extent UUs believe in such things, our ideas are far from the conventional understandings of these terms. Religious notions of sin and evil have typically served the purpose of orienting human behavior and framing the human condition. Behavior that is discouraged is categorized as sinful. Realities of the human condition that are undesirable are deemed evil. Yet, religions have typically taken similar experiences and arrived at widely divergent conclusions with regard to what is deemed sinful or evil. What might be considered sinful or evil from a Hindu perspective can be quite different when examined through the lenses of Protestantism. Similarly, the historical Unitarian and Universalist perspectives on these terms has differed from that of mainstream American Protestantism.

New England Puritanism, out of which both Unitarianism and Universalism emerged, subscribed to the Calvinist belief in original sin. This belief held that all humans are born into a condition of inherent sinfulness. A combination of faith and leading a good life was required in order to be saved from this inherent sinfulness by God. According to the most severe Puritan interpretations, even piety and proper conduct did not guarantee election; the elect were chosen by God's inscrutable grace alone, which mere human action was powerless to influence. The process of determining who was among the elect became increasingly complicated and convoluted as Puritanism took firmer hold in American soil. Eventually, dissent against the Puritan (Calvinist) notions of original sin and election began to emerge, fueled by liberal religious thinking in Europe.

The Congregationalist Churches of New England, the heirs of the Puritan tradition, began to experience a theological rift between more traditional, conservative ministers and those with increasingly liberal ideals. Liberal Congregationalists, the forerunners of the Unitarian movement, became associated with a theology known as Arminianism, the belief that people are born with the capacity for both sin and goodness and that salvation is possible for all.[16]

Our Unitarian forebears, in proposing that humans can choose between good and evil, developed a theology with greater emphasis on the actions people take. Universalists, with their doctrine of universal salvation, faced a complicated question: If all were eventually saved anyway, then why even try to lead a "good life" in the here and now? The Universalists developed different ways of answering this question, tending to emphasize that although universal salvation eventually happened for all, one was likely to be saved more quickly by leading a good life. The Universalists explicitly included an emphasis on good deeds in their 1803 Winchester Profession.

There are very strong connections between these historical theological developments and contemporary Unitarian Universalism. Present-day UUs continue to disagree with those who view evil or sinfulness as an inherent, God-given state of being. While recognizing human finitude, UUs are far more likely to characterize people's actions or inactions as good or bad, placing a continued emphasis on deeds and individual choice. Although UUs have been chastened by the events of the past century, we still tend to be optimistic and to believe that human commitment and energy can change many of the wrongs in the world. In this lies not only individual salvation but the potential salvation of all humanity and perhaps of the earth itself. Sin and evil, in the current UU conception, thus tend to be viewed as the result of both human actions and failures. Yet the solution, or salvation, as it were, also lies largely in the hands of individuals—in the cultivation of character leading to positive actions—strengthening individuals' potential to be positive forces in the world.

Although UUs have been chastened by the events of the past century, we still tend to be optimistic and to believe that human commitment and energy can change many of the wrongs in the world.

How Do We View Human Nature?

With typical UU theological bias, the Commission did not ask questions about the nature of sin and evil, nor did any respondent mention these concepts in core of faith statements. However, among the statements considered most important by all groups surveyed is this one: *Humans are born with the potential to be good; we are committed to nurturing good through love and learning.* Around 90 percent of lay respondents and ministers considered this highly important. While there was little variation among lay respondents, among ministers this affirmation was particularly valued by women, feeling personality types, and those under age forty-five.

First written for the Berry Street Conference in 1941, UU theologian James Luther Adams's essay on "The Changing Reputation of Human Nature" captures something of the tension of the time within the Unitarian tradition and is relevant to UU self-understanding today. Adams reflected upon three views of human nature, two from Greek philosophy and a third from Christianity, that he believed combined the other two. The first view asserts that "reason is the masterful principle of creation. . . . Man's primary, distinguishing faculty is his reason, and through it he can release a vitality that will enable him to achieve control of himself and of the human situation."[17] This view "exalts the cognitive, non-affective aspects of the human psyche." The second perspective views existence "more in terms of . . . a vitality that is both creative and destructive, that imbues every form but that also eludes and bursts the bounds of every structure." This point of view Adams referred to as voluntarism, because it focuses on will—vitality, feelings, and choice-making—rather than reason as the key to understanding human nature. He saw these two views as coming together in Christianity. Adams understood the intellectualism of his era as a reaction to "extreme forms of voluntarism."[18] However, his essay warns that the rationalistic tradition of his time

Does the UU understanding of human nature do justice to its complexity and to motivations for personal and social transformation?

> has optimistically taken for granted the idea of unity in the world . . . and in the structure of the individual psyche. . . . [It] stresses the role of reason in such a way as to offer a truncated view of the functions operative in both society and the individual and also in such a way as to encourage both separative individualism and "the attitude of distance." The voluntaristic outlook . . . aims to correct and supplement this view.[19]

The liberal optimism Adams spoke of was soon to be curtailed by history, but the question remains: Does the UU understanding of human nature do justice to its complexity and to motivations for personal and social transformation?

From our Universalist, voluntarist side comes the statement *We embrace a covenant in love not to "give up on anyone"—to create inclusive community,* which was affirmed by 80 percent of lay respondents and 72 percent of clergy as highly important.

The challenge of a UU doctrine of human nature, according to Meadville Lombard professor Thandeka, is that the Unitarians had one idea (shaped by William Ellery Channing) and the Universalists had another (shaped by Hosea Ballou); when the two denominations consolidated in 1961, this and other differences were never resolved. Thandeka traces in the formative events of each theologian's life the vision of human nature he expressed in his theologies, one more rationalistic, the other more voluntaristic:

Channing affirmed an independent, disembodied mind—an autonomous self—as the essence of human nature. Ballou affirmed an interrelational self, one in which the feelings of the human body co-determine the state of the human mind. Channing believed human identity was completely discrete. For Ballou, it was embodied and thus communal because the body cannot exist without environmental support.[20]

Out of Ballou's worldview, then, comes this question: To what extent do UUs' theological and philosophical differences reflect our efforts to make sense of the formative experiences of our lives?

Some who embrace a covenant of inclusive community are inspired by the vision of Ballou and other Universalists of a God who keeps the latch-string out until the last child comes home. Carl Scovel, former minister of King's Chapel in Boston, offers his story:

> What changed *my* life . . . was my own discovery, or the divine disclosure, that I, who trusted least, could trust this love, that I, who believed so little, could believe it, that I, who wished to be above all self-sufficient, could receive it, that in my own imperfect way I could even sometimes live a little bit of it; and that I could do this, not because I was good, moral, clever, or wise, but because that love, that good intent at life's own center, was beginning to transform me, not as I expected (god's other name, after all, is surprise) but most surely and most steadily.[21]

Do We Believe in a Transcendent Dimension?

Among the nearly eight hundred UUs who provided the Commission with a statement of what is at the core of their personal faith, between 16 and 30 percent of respondents from diverse groups named a transcendent dimension, whether or not they called it God. Quite a few respondents found a powerful center of faith in "deepening my response to God's inexhaustible love." One wrote, "At center is and always has been a rooted, personal, and living sense of connection to 'source,' 'the Eternal,' what as a child I was taught to name God. But even then I knew it was much bigger than humans can name." Individual Christian UUs offer statements embracing "belief in God and Universal salvation for all souls" and "the importance of Jesus as an inspirational focus." Several respondents expressed a strong opinion to the contrary: "The core of my faith is that there is no God."

"The depth dimension of our lives (spirituality) calls us to live mindfully, seek meaning, and serve love." Close to 90 percent of survey respondents gave this affirmation high importance. Women rated the statement higher

than did men. It is of considerable interest that 86 percent of lay respondents and 90 percent of clergy valued both *spirituality* and *reason*.

Knowing and experiencing come together in spirituality, what minister Nancy Arnold calls "that elusive term that almost defies definition." She continues,

> Spirituality points, always, beyond: beyond the ordinary, beyond possession, beyond the narrow confines of the self, and—above all—beyond expectation. Because "the spiritual" is beyond our control, it is never exactly what we expect. . . . Carl Jung . . . remarked that "one of the main functions of formalized religion is to protect people against a direct experience of God."[22]

Humanist minister Khoren Arisian offers these words:

> To learn to be in touch with this fundamental life force, this depth dimension of reality that cannot be weighed or measured, is to sanctify one's existence, and, through its working out, to establish the grounds for lasting affection between people and the earth at-large. It's the kind of love that never diminishes, ever grows, and makes all things new.[23]

"We encounter 'God' in our own depths, in others, and in nature, seeking wholeness and transformation." This statement, too, reflects a broad consensus among UUs. Even in a congregation with a strong humanist identity, 80 percent rated this statement important. Among respondents, there was a positive correlation with Feeling personality types and younger age. One GA participant wrote, "I believe in God, but not in the traditional sense. For me, God is the organizing force of the Universe, the rays of sun that shine through breaking clouds on the horizon, and most importantly, that which gives existence to all kinds of love between living beings."

Ministers who value naturalistic "god" language, as exemplified by the above quotation, tend to rate relationality and community highly: "My faith is in the abiding presence of God which I find in all living things. This presence is the spark of love which animates us, sustains us." UU minister Gary Kowalski writes in *Science and the Search for God*, "God is in the details—the lavishness and extravagance that bless every niche, nook and cranny of creation, so that out of the millions of species who inhabit our globe, not one creature has been left half-painted, merely sketched in or without a role to play within the larger picture."[24]

"'God' can be conceived as a pervasive Creativity, ever evolving, that lures us beyond our limiting horizons." Process theism was more controversial among lay respondents. About 60 percent of lay respondents considered

this concept highly important; 82 percent of ministers did. Among ministers, correlations reflect both the relational and creative emphases of process theology. Richard Gilbert, a mystical humanist, explained,

> With Henry Nelson Wieman, I think of the divine as the power of cosmic creativity. That creativity is manifest in nature as creative evolution; it is observed in history in those prophets of the human spirit who have tried to bend the arc of history toward justice against all odds; it is manifest here and now as we are co-creators of the Beloved Community. . . . It is my mystic identification with this creative process that prompts me to continue."[25]

"Spiritual reality engages us in the midst of paradox and mystery; we are challenged to abide there at times." This statement was also preferred by ministers over lay informants by a similar ratio of about four to three. "I dwell at the center of Mystery, possibility. To awaken to love and compassion, and to grow in wisdom are my central tasks," wrote one minister. Another found his center in "faith in the compassion of God in the midst of paradox & mystery." A GA participant who saw exploring what holds us together as the "most important issue we face today" wrote, "I use the word God, but it represents the unknown or mystery in life to me."

Similarly, 58 percent of lay respondents said that they have had mystical experiences, compared to 81 percent of clergy. Most such experiences fall under the heading of natural mysticism. Examples include a profound sense of oneness with nature or with people, the birth of a child or the death of a loved one, something enfolding or uniting all things, a sudden new insight imbued with a feeling of certainty. For some, such compelling experiences have shaped the major choices of their lives.

Many people who shared their perspectives with the Commission find their religious lives in the creative space between theological positions, taking a "both . . . and" approach to religious labels. Minister Richard Gilbert writes,

> By *mystic* I mean one sensitive to a reality greater than the self, but of which the self is an integral part. Believing self is enmeshed in ultimate reality, the mystic celebrates that serendipitous union. . . . I try imaginatively to take a "God's eye view of the world," seeking to distance myself, however slightly, from my humanist perspective, to identify with the highest cosmic good insofar as I can imagine that good. In that sense I am a mystic, with a prophetic twist.[26]

Minister Lex Crane argues for *rational mysticism* at the core of UU religion:

Many people who shared their perspectives with the Commission find their religious lives in the creative space between theological positions, taking a "both . . . and" approach to religious labels.

The rational perspective divides reality into discreet parts . . . and gives a name to each part so that it can be held in the mind, be expressed in speech. . . . The mystical world view does just the reverse. It sets aside all words, all concepts or divisions, and perceives the world as one unified whole, radiant with meaning, and oneself set down in it, an integral part of it all. . . . If we learn to perceive the world now through mystical eyes and then, at other times, from a rational perspective, we begin to approach seeing the world whole. We get closer to reality. To God.[27]

What Are Our Spiritual Paths?

How does the widely recognized interest in spirituality express itself? Scott Alexander's *Everyday Spiritual Practice: Simple Pathways for Enriching Your Life* offers some examples in a number of essays by Unitarian Universalists. Alexander describes "everyday spiritual practice" as "any activity or attitude in which you can regularly and intentionally engage, and which significantly deepens the quality of your relationship with the miracle of life both within and beyond you."[28]

Respondents to the Commission's theology questionnaire were asked about the importance in their lives of four paths: the path of *love* and *service* (engaging the will), the path of *community* (engaging the heart), the path of *understanding* (engaging the mind), and the path of *interior harmony* (engaging body and soul). All four were solidly supported among lay respondents (around 70 percent rated each highly important). Interestingly, the first two proved most important to ministers (at 92 and 82 percent, respectively, compared to 62 and 58 percent for the second pair). Here are some responses from workshop and questionnaire participants, as well as writers who find each important:

If we learn to perceive the world now through mystical eyes and then, at other times, from a rational perspective, we begin to approach seeing the world whole.

Love and Service
- One minister found her congregation's core to be "the ethic of Jesus: love and service, fed by direct experience of awe and wonder of ourselves and others in worship."
- Marilyn Sewell, a minister in Portland, Oregon, writes,

> Only one kind of religion counts today, and that is the kind which is radical enough to engage in the world's basic troubles. If it cannot do that, then it can do nothing which merits our concern or the world's respect. . . . Transformation will occur when we dare to stop talking about social concerns and actually move to alleviate real human pain.[29]

Community

- One respondent found his faith core in being "gently and inclusively guided toward beloved community."
- A second saw the core as "yearning for connections and a just and peaceful community and world, and a sense that through community we touch something larger than ourselves."
- Another described her congregation's faith core as being "believers of and in Community."
- Meadville Lombard professor David Bumbaugh challenges us:

> It will not be enough to offer people the opportunity to "build your own theology." They must be offered the freedom to build their own theology in the context of a community which is asking serious and probing religious questions, and has the courage to make deep and profound affirmations—questions and affirmations rooted in a sense of who we are and what we care profoundly about.[30]

Understanding

- A respondent described the core of his faith as being "taught by my church and parents that I need to think for myself, study and learn, draw my own conclusions, and be responsible for my own actions and their consequences. I have followed this, and continue to believe what my mind and experience tell me I must."
- Another found his core in "the God of my understanding."
- Philosopher Ken Wilbur points out,

> Though all of the contemplative traditions aim at going within and beyond reason, they all *start* with reason, start with the notion that truth is to be established by *evidence*, that truth is the result of *experimental* methods, that truth is to be *tested* in the laboratory of personal experience . . . and that dogmas or given beliefs are precisely what hinder the emergence of deeper truths and wider visions.[31]

Interior Harmony

- One minister commented that for younger people, "living in harmony with nature and living simply (lightly on the earth)" are core, while the older generation focuses more on "human potential."
- Minister Barbara Carlson writes,

> It was not until I began a daily practice of meditation and in the deep silence fell smack dab into my own shadow—all the rationalizations, justifications, intellectualizations used over the years to maintain my "good girl" self-image—that I truly began to heal, truly began to learn the meaning of compassion.[32]

Who Has Inspired Us?

This question produced a wide range of responses. After their own families, ministers, teachers, and friends, people most often named Jesus and the Buddha as sources of inspiration. James Luther Adams came second to Jesus among ministers, followed by the Buddha. Members of the laity also mentioned, in order of frequency, Gandhi, Martin Luther King Jr., the Dalai Lama, Ralph Waldo Emerson, Bertrand Russell, Deepak Chopra, Wayne Dyer, William Ellery Channing, William Schulz, and Kahlil Gibran. Ministers left out Russell, Chopra, and Dyer and added Thich Nhat Hanh, Rebecca Parker, Howard Thurman, Rumi, Henry Nelson Wieman, Joanna Macy, Matthew Fox, and Starhawk. Eclectic as this list is, there were many more. The limited number of UU forebears among lay responses is noteworthy. How might we address this?

How Have We Changed?

Many respondents supported the general observation that there has been a shift in Unitarian Universalism away from a humanist center to a more eclectic mix of philosophies or theologies.

Many respondents supported the general observation that there has been a shift in Unitarian Universalism away from a humanist center to a more eclectic mix of philosophies or theologies. This finding is additionally supported by the comments of a number of search committees that submitted packets in the past few years. Some fear this trend, while others celebrate it. Among the ministers surveyed, 39 percent said their congregations had become "more spiritual," 26 percent "more diverse," 19 percent "less humanistic," and 15 percent more comfortable with "religious" language.

But people have noted other shifts as well, among them a growing awareness of "right relations" in congregations and a stronger sense of mission and inclusiveness. About 13 percent said there had been no change. Only 5 percent said their congregation had become "more theistic." There was mention of "new age" attitudes not always tested by an inquiring mind, but for the most part it appears UUs are attempting a holistic integration, using human experience as the primary authority across theological leanings as they are reflected upon through dialogue in community.

Theological Challenges

As the Commission explored what might make up a Unitarian Universalist theological profile, we encountered areas of challenge as well as common ground and creative tension. While this is not the place for an extensive discussion of such challenges, we reflect briefly here upon several areas that are pertinent to UU self-understanding: challenges to Enlightenment philosophy, a postmodern critique of the modernist worldview, dealing with our Christian roots, challenges to Romanticism's fascination with the exotic, and the dilemma of spiritual depth versus breadth.

Outgrowing the Enlightenment Worldview

John Cobb, liberal Christian process theologian, was asked as a sympathetic outsider to give his observations about Unitarian Universalism:

> Today the limitations of Enlightenment modes of thought and of social organization are becoming more and more apparent. Whereas progress in the past two centuries has meant increasing the role of Enlightenment principles in our religious life, today it means something quite different. The dualism, the individualism, the rationalism, and the empiricism of the Enlightenment have all failed us. . . .
>
> Unitarian Universalists have freed themselves from pre-Enlightenment baggage precisely by committing themselves to the insights of the Enlightenment. But now it is just those partial truths whose exaltation in theory and practice is destroying us. Can Unitarian Universalists find the resources to criticize the principles by which they have lived? If so, where? . . .
>
> If Unitarian Universalists could become self-critical in this way, you could once again be in the vanguard of dealing with the most important issues of our time. I do not expect this, but I hope for it.[33]

Unitarianism in particular claims strong roots in the Enlightenment. Its gifts are enduring: reason—a valuing of evidence and the scientific method; tolerance—the possibility of valuing multiple perspectives; and freedom—an appreciation of introspection, autonomy, and individual vs. role identity (which prepared the ground for such movements as women's suffrage). The Enlightenment moved humans out of the center of the universe and encouraged imaginative possibility.[34] Now we need to ask ourselves if it is possible that we have identified too strongly with a particular worldview and philosophical era. Could a continuing evolution of worldviews leave UUs holding the rearguard instead of the front lines at this time in history?

The modern world is struggling with an increased pace of change and the challenge of new paradigms. Many people are coping by trying to return to ways that worked in the past. Unitarian process theologian Henry Nelson Wieman's definition of evil is resistance—resistance to change, resistance to the flow of creativity.[35] Yet how do we know when it is time to let go, and when is the new idea on the horizon simply a passing fad that does not contribute to human wholeness? The hunger for more spirituality many UUs are expressing may well be a response to the lure of an emerging era.

The Postmodern Critique

Postmodernism is a reaction against or a corrective to modernism. Modernism in theology can be very broadly characterized as a worldview based on an optimistic faith in progress and the rational pursuit of knowledge. Postmodern thinking, by contrast, asserts that it is hard to predict whether science will eventually save the world or destroy it.

In the nineteenth century, certain thinkers and philosophers such as Friedrich Nietzsche became disillusioned with the idea that knowledge could be objective and absolute. Nietzsche asserted that everything we know comes to us with a bias, our own and that of the predominant culture, and that how we know things is entangled in all kinds of social constructs. In the twentieth century, Jacques Derrida took this idea one step further, proposing a method of examining knowledge as it is expressed through written texts, what he called *deconstruction*.[36] Derrida asserted that for any text there are multiple conflicting interpretations, none of which is definitive—everything is capable of holding multiple meanings.

Author Daniel Adams says that postmodernism is a reaction to modern Western culture, in particular its excesses, arrogance, and ethnocentrism. He sees deconstructive postmodernism as a transitional viewpoint, composed as it is of negations of that which came before. He calls the postmodern age an in-between time: "The postmodern is the name given to this space between what was and what is yet to be."[37] There are, however, a number of thinkers in North America who look positively at the "constructive" school of postmodernism.

Adams points out that one of the most significant trends of modern culture, the secularization of society, is starting to be reversed. Partly this is because the "false gods" that replaced theism (he names communism, nationalism, and progress as examples) have clearly failed, and people feel the need for something to take their place. He identifies four characteristics of postmodern thinking:

- A decline of the Western worldview, which is based on progress, science, democracy, and individual rights. This worldview, when imposed on non-Western societies, came with a sense of cultural arrogance, an assumption that the modern Western way is the best way in all instances. The erosion of faith in democracy and individuality can clearly go in positive or negative directions. But if postmodernism questions the viability of a belief in the absolute autonomy of the individual, could it not be nudging us in the direction of a more interconnected sense of life? Could it not bring us to the interdependent web of all existence of which we are a part?

- A crisis of legitimization. If the worldviews that previously held sway are no longer considered authoritative, what is? Where others see a negative outcome in terms of relativism and syncretism, Adams sees a growing plurality of values.

- The creation of a new intellectual marketplace. Access to knowledge is no longer controlled by an academic or cultural elite. This means a far more diverse chorus of ideas and interpretations, all of which have equal claims to validity.

- Deconstruction. As Adams puts it, "Objective truth is replaced by hermeneutic truth," or truth that needs to emerge in the process of interpreting our experience. This too leads to intellectual pluralism.

Suzanne Meyer, in her lecture to the Minister's Convocation in Birmingham, Alabama, in 2002, applied these concepts to Unitarian Universalism. She pointed out that in many ways we are the quintessential modern religion—based on those Enlightenment ideals of rationalism, individuality, and faith in science and progress. She agrees with Adams that postmodernism critiques the blind spots and biases of modernism and affirms that it remains a needed perspective. She, like Adams, understands postmodernism as a "between time" approach. Modernity is losing ground, but as yet nothing, at least nothing comforting or comfortable, has emerged to replace it.

Meyers uses the metaphor of the Exodus to explain where Unitarian Universalists are in this process. We were perfectly comfortable, she says, in Egypt. We are probably not comfortable in the wilderness:

There is always the possibility that we may perish in the desert, that our religious movement is so inextricably wedded to modernism that it will not survive long enough to make it to the Promised Land. And although we are the generation that left Egypt, I seriously doubt we will be the ones to enter the promise. Nevertheless, brothers and sisters, we will have an important role to play as faithful and decisive leaders during this nomadic time.[38]

Many of the words used by the authors to talk about the postmodern world—*pluralistic, radically inclusive, syncretic*—are the very words we could use to describe contemporary Unitarian Universalism. A familiarity with postmodern thought can help UUs to understand our own evolution as a movement. An attempt to call the UU movement back to a time when there was an easy and identifiable core, a single overarching paradigm, would be a move backward instead of forward. According to author Leonard Sweet, "Postmodern thought has turned with a vengeance against Enlightenment notions of a fixed center toward which we strive, or a single central self."[39] So as UUs seek the core of their faith, they should be careful not to settle for an anachronistic or nostalgic vision of what Unitarian Universalism was in the past rather than a dynamic vision of what it is and will be, or should be.

Our Christian Roots

Both the Unitarian and the Universalist national organizations were Christian at the time of consolidation, although this seems to have been forgotten or ignored in some parts of the denomination. In the intervening forty-two years, there has been a dramatic shift. Today most UUs, if asked, "Are you Christian?" would respond with something between "Well, not really," and "Hell, no!" Though there are many UU Christians, they have become a minority within the denomination. In fact, UUs seem almost proud of the way they have abandoned their roots. "We are not Christian," some say, perhaps implying that they are better than Christian, that they have moved beyond Christianity. In religious studies, this idea is called *supersessionism*; one example is the notion that Christianity superseded Judaism. Now many of us imply that Unitarian Universalism has superseded Christianity.

Unitarian Universalists need to make peace with their heritage.

We are not suggesting, as some might, that Unitarian Universalism should become a Christian denomination again. That would not be remotely practical, even if it were desirable. But UUs should do a better job of remembering the tradition from which they came, and even be grateful to it. UUs should be aware of, and make use of, the rich gifts the movement's heritage has for them. UUs need to stop being afraid to talk about their roots.

There are two aspects to this idea. *Individually*, UUs need to make peace with their own religious backgrounds, whatever they may be. In completely throwing away the religion of one's childhood, one loses a lot. This includes people who were raised in a rigid, dogmatic faith—the ones we usually think of as having serious issues with their past—but also others. For example, it includes born-and-raised UUs who may have issues with the humanism they were exposed to in childhood. As a contrary example, there is a rich mystical tradition in humanism, including among many of those who drafted the original Humanist Manifesto, that is often overlooked by humanists today.

We strongly encourage all UUs to be intentional about dealing with their past. It is important, of course, to do things only as they are appropriate and not charge into painful psychic territory before one is ready. But we strongly caution against getting stuck in a place of comfortable reactivity, and never moving past it.

Institutionally, Unitarian Universalism needs to make peace with its Christian heritage. While there are many strands of UU heritage about which people are ignorant, Christianity is what tends to make people reactive. This

Unitarian Universalist need to stop being afraid to talk about their roots.

makes sense based on UU demographics—the largest number of "wounded" come-inners have come from Christian faiths, and so they tend to react against that tradition. But although Unitarian Universalism is not a Christian faith today, within living memory it was, and its roots are firmly in the Christian tradition. Just as a person loses a lot by throwing away his or her personal religious past, UUs also collectively lose a great deal of who we are and what we could be by discarding the entirety of this part of our heritage. As long we continue to allow this reactivity to Christianity to disconnect us from our personal and institutional heritage, we will be lacking a large part of who we are as a movement and will be unable to be fully whole.

Exoticism

The diversity of spiritual and scriptural sources available to Unitarian Universalists is a source of intense pride for most. It is a mark of the undogmatic nature of the faith, and of the fact that UUs can find many ways to express the core spiritual values we hold dear. However, as the adage goes, one's greatest strength can also be one's greatest weakness. The spiritual and scriptural openness of the UU faith, which appeals to so many, also creates some unique problems. One such problem, which is also related to the ambivalence (or outright hostility) many UUs feel toward their personal religious roots, is that of cultural and religious misappropriation and exoticism.

The problem of exoticism is rooted in the background of most adult UUs as well as prevailing cultural notions of what's fashionable. The vast majority of UUs are come-inners, those who were not raised in the religion and came to it as converts. (A 1997 denomination study showed that at the time, only 10 percent of members had been raised in UU traditions.) The vast majority of these converts, in turn, are UUs who were either unchurched or previously churched in the Christian or Jewish traditions. Those who left their Christian congregations usually did so because of some sense of disaffection or incompatibility. Many UUs in this come-inner category have not completely processed or reconciled their feelings of dissatisfaction with the religion they have left behind. Those unreconciled feelings tend to manifest themselves in the form of a strong reaction against anything that draws on the religious traditions they have abandoned. For the unreconciled, the use of Christian scripture or metaphor in UU services tends to raise suspicion and sometimes anger.

This undercurrent of anti-Christianity is reinforced by cultural sentiments among the liberal intellectuals Unitarian Universalism tends to attract that Christianity is passé. It's old news; it's too conservative; it has been co-opted by people opposed to the values religious liberals hold dear. In short, it's not "in." What is "in," and also unobjectionable (from the standpoint of many unreconciled former Christians), is anything Eastern or "earthy" in nature. Hinduism, Buddhism, Native American spirituality, and pagan earth-centered religions have been identified as trendy, cool, and acceptable among UUs.

The problem with this is that the fashionability of these "exotic" religions is frequently defined in opposition to Christianity. The exotic religions are *prima facie* given great latitude and not always critically examined, while any use of Christian sources in UU churches is minutely scrutinized. There is an unspoken assumption that Christian sources need to be treated with suspicion, while other, more exotic sources are inherently full of wisdom. In truth, as most of our UU clergy are aware, there is as much wisdom and insight in Jewish and Christian sources as there is in other more fashionable traditions.

This exotic fashionability of non-Judeo-Christian sources is something that the UU movement has not adequately examined but needs to. There is a colonialist attitude inherent in the way UUs, made up predominantly of whites, seem to pick and choose what they want from religions that have traditionally belonged to ethnic groups different from the majority UU demographic. It seems like an unspoken assumption that UUs, as members of a predominatly white denomination, can take what we find appealing from the religions of Native Americans, East Asians, South Asians, and others without any regard for the context or the history of the symbols, beliefs, and practices that we are seeking to co-opt. (One small example of this is the universal depiction in UU circles of Buddhism as a religion of peace and nonviolence, an image that does not stand the test of history. One need merely examine the histories of Sri Lanka and Cambodia to understand that.)

The reality is that all religions have their flaws and have been historically misused. While UUs are hypersensitive to this reality when it comes to Christianity, we are virtually uncritical in our examination of religions considered exotic. This exoticism, when examined through the lenses of white power, raises concerns over how Unitarian Universalists, as a movement, might be adopting the symbols, rituals, and beliefs of traditionally nonwhite religions in a way that is tokenizing (selectively picking and choosing), in essence a form of cultural misappropriation that could be interpreted as racist. To the extent that the process of appropriation typically occurs in an uncritical vacuum or with a lack of full contextual understanding, UUs run the additional risk of misappropriating (taking out of context) that which we are adopting as our own.

A particular aspect of this issue concerns religious language. Because of the almost instinctive resistance to all things Christian, which has become a strong undercurrent in the UU movement, it tends to be quite difficult for ministers to use English-language theological terms rooted in Christianity. Terms like *sin*, *redemption*, *salvation*, and even *God* require elaborate

The exotic religions are given great latitude and not always critically examined, while any use of Christian sources in UU churches is minutely scrutinized.

explanation and redefinition when used in a UU context. Even then, some UUs still object, arguing that these terms have already been defined by mainstream Christianity and cannot be redefined. Many of these same UUs will uncritically accept the use of terms like *nirvana*, *dharma*, *karma*, or *moksha* from the UU pulpit, even though our own usage of these terms almost invariably requires some measure of redefinition or reinterpretation. Again, the exotic gets a pass, while the familiar (that which may have caused hurt in the past) is heavily scrutinized. Even in terms of the theological language to which UUs tend to be open, we see themes of racial/cultural power and appropriation at play.

To be clear, we are not arguing that UUs should turn away from the spiritual wisdom they have found in Hinduism, Buddhism, Native American spirituality, earth-centered religions, and other traditions. UUs could, however, probably benefit from a deeper examination of how we relate to all of the religious traditions we currently draw on. If we can find ways to do this, we can move as a movement toward a more holistic approach to our diverse theological sources. If we begin addressing these problems we stand to achieve a deeper, more authentic understanding of all the spiritual and scriptural sources available to us.

Depth versus Breadth

One great challenge for Unitarian Universalism is the issue of depth versus breadth. As we become ever more inclusive, as the circle widens ever more broadly, we court the danger of becoming "a mile wide and an inch deep." UUs have been charged with this on more than one occasion.

Unitarian Universalists love variety. And yet, if spiritual development—whatever that means—requires discipline, attention, and time, then it also requires focus. In this way it is comparable to academics: one can be an expert in one area and have a general idea about many others, but to know a subject thoroughly is to become specialized. Spirituality is not academics, but something similar is true of it. It is not possible to walk all paths at once. Religion scholar Huston Smith makes exactly this point:

> The problem with cafeteria-style spirituality is that Saint Ego is often the one making the choices at the salad bar. What tastes good is not always the same as what you need, and an undeveloped ego can make unwise choices. I believe that it is most helpful for people to choose one main meal, to commit and focus on that tradition, and then to add to it if the need arises. I am a firm believer in vitamin supplements. [40]

Without rejecting the respectful borrowing of elements from other tra-

Unitarian Universalists love variety. And yet, if spiritual development requires discipline, attention, and time, then it also requires focus.

ditions, there is merit to Smith's suggestion that they should be supplements and spices and not the main course. Other traditions should not be used as distractions from Unitarian Universalism's own path. Pieces from other traditions can illuminate and enrich the UU tradition, but they cannot in themselves make up that tradition. Too often, it seems, UUs try to achieve just that.

But what about those for whom their "other" discipline is their primary religious path? Perhaps if we had more to offer within Unitarian Universalism, they might not feel such a need to go elsewhere.

This is not to say that it is wrong to be a UU and pursue a discipline from another tradition. The numbers indicate that it is certainly possible to be a "hyphenated UU," and to follow a particular spiritual discipline within the community and values of Unitarian Universalism. Nor does this mean there should be an orthodox UU path that is imposed from outside or that is supposed to fit for everyone. However, perhaps it would be beneficial if UUs had their own distinctly UU spiritual path, something we could use to explore our own depths and increase our depth of spiritual exploration, without having to go outside the UU faith.

The Ground on Which We Meet

"Since we embrace theological diversity," wrote one respondent to the Commission's question, "it is our living historical tradition and its imperative for the future that is at the core of our faith." Professor David Bumbaugh, who finds his center "between Kenneth Patton's mystical humanism and Henry Nelson Wieman's natural theism," offers this vision:

> The heart of a faith for the twenty-first century, I am convinced, is suggested by the seventh Principle. . . . Hidden in this apparently uncomplicated, uncontroversial, innocuous statement is a radical theological position. The seventh Principle calls us to reverence before the world, not some future world, but this miraculous world of our everyday experience. It challenges us to understand the world as reflexive and relational rather than hierarchical. It bespeaks a world in which neither god nor humanity is at the center; in which the center is the void, the ever fecund matrix out of which being emerges. . . . It calls us to trust the process, the creative, evolving, renewing, redeeming process which brings us into being, which sustains us in being, and which transforms our being. It offers a vision of a world in which the holy, the sacred is incarnated in every moment, in every aspect of being, a world in which God is always fully present, and in which God is always fully at risk.[41]

Can our congregations be places where the world finds itself open to the in-breaking of new life? Charlotte Shivvers, retired minister and social activist, suggests as much: "The very emptiness that is left in that central place is neither weakness nor failure. It can become a place of humility, acceptance, and wonder—and a place where we all can meet."[42]

These images have sparked provocative discussions among the commissioners, as we hope they will among our readers. Words like *emptiness* and *void* mean radically different things to us. Three years of study and conversation have not brought us to a complete consensus about a common core to our faith. Yet we have found much common ground along the way, in the material we share here.

In reflecting upon underlying unities, this report has for the most part resisted the tendency to sort UUs into theological boxes. As retired minister Phillip Hewett writes,

> It's pretty hard, sometimes, to follow through consistently with a refusal to accept labels which assign you to one or another of mutually exclusive camps, desiccating the richness of human response to the overall reality we experience into a few hard and fast categories. . . . I am not interested in trying to sort people out into categories. The categories I have in mind . . . coexist and interact within our tradition—and, whether we care to admit it or not, they coexist and interact within each one of us, in widely varying proportions and ways.[43]

Given that UUs do name themselves so diversely, what do postmodern UU Christians, new humanists, Buddhist UUs, process theologians and religious naturalists, UUs who embrace earth-centered pagan practices, advocates of liberation and feminist theologies, and UU mystics of all stripes have in common? In what ways are the diverse flavors of the UU tradition moving toward shared understanding while retaining their own particular wisdom and practice? What gifts does each bring that are distinctive and creatively challenge UUs? What vision can UUs hold that, while honoring these gifts, binds them together to pursue a common future?

Do all the diverse Unitarian Universalists stand upon any shared theological ground? Respecting the integrity of individual perspective, we offer the following statements as descriptive of who Unitarian Universalists are theologically:

We are a grounded faith. We are a faith with roots, however lightly held, that go back two thousand years and more. Unlike other more recently evolving nontraditional faiths, ours is solidly grounded in both the realm of history and the realm of ideas.

In what ways are the diverse flavors of the UU tradition moving toward shared understanding while retaining their own particular wisdom and practice?

We are an ecological faith. The "interdependent web" concept of our seventh Principle is not new to history (the "net of Indra" in Hindu and Buddhist thought has been around for several thousand years). But in the West this vision of interconnectedness has had an uphill struggle to displace a more hierarchical vision of the nature of the cosmos. We have placed the web squarely at the center of our shared worldview.

We are a profoundly human faith. Whether we see our charge as loving our neighbor or ending the suffering of all sentient beings, whether a transcendent dimension is part of our worldview or not, our primary focus for religious action is the well-being of this world. We wrestle with our ideas about human limitation and human power and acknowledge that our understandings are imperfect.

We are a responsible faith. At our best, we are able to respond to our deep sense of interconnectedness with both the natural and human worlds. Whatever our source of religious inspiration, we understand that humanity must take its responsibility for the state of the world seriously. We humans have created many of the ills from which we and all creatures on this planet suffer. We have the ability to ameliorate suffering, if only we find the will to do so. Our diverse sources of religious inspiration power our will to act.

We are an experiential faith. We are focused more on experience (our own and that of trusted others, past and present) than beliefs. We do not hold with beliefs that contradict our experience, although we recognize that there are realities that can draw us beyond the present limits of our knowledge.

We are a free faith. We are free both as individuals and as congregations. We recognize the authenticity and integrity of each individual's life journey, and concepts such as "building your own theology" or "composing a faith" resonate with us. We are a faith of heretics (from the Greek *hairesis*, "to choose").

We are an imaginative faith. We engage with image and story, garnering wisdom from many traditions and building bridges between them, making a place where creativity can flourish.

We are a relational faith. While we support the individual journey, we ground it in caring community. Relational language occurs more frequently than any other in core-of-faith statements shared with the Commission. *We are a covenantal faith.* We are held together, from our Reformation roots, by our chosen commitment to each other rather than by creed, ecclesiastical authority, or revealed truth. We began to reclaim that heritage with the language of our Principles. More recently, we have come to recognize ourselves as a dialogical faith; the explosion of covenant groups in

We have the ability to ameliorate suffering, if only we find the will to do so. Our diverse sources of religious inspiration power our will to act.

our midst reflects this. We are reminded of Francis David's admonition over four centuries ago: "We need not think alike to love alike."

We are a curious faith. Freedom and tolerance have been central to our tradition at least since the Reformation. The psychological characteristics and values of people drawn to our ranks suggest openness is a compelling characteristic, even if we do not always live our values of tolerance, acceptance, and respect as well as we might. We acknowledge that our perspective is limited, that we could be wrong, that we live in the midst of uncertainties, yet we are ever open to new insights.

We are a reasonable faith. We do not ask people to check their rationality at the door, and we encourage the practice of disciplined inquiry toward personal and societal assumptions. We challenge idolatries, especially our own. We are positive toward the findings of science, while questioning the values that at times motivate choices in that area as in every other.

We are a hopeful faith. We are a faith of possibilities, aspiring to be (though we often fall short) a transformative faith, a justice-seeking faith. We would create a space for the realization of possibility, whether we call it the "commonwealth of God" or the "Beloved Community."

A powerful vision! And one that can be claimed by all strands of the UU tradition. At the same time, UUs should not lose sight of the critiques mirrored by the more newly visible strands in the UU web of community. For theological concerns surface organically when they are called forth by the cry of the heart and the need of the world; these strands are growing because the times call for what they offer.

Neopaganism reminds UUs that we would do well to become a more *embodied faith*, respecting the power of ritual and the importance of beauty, living more fully in our individual and corporate bodies and therefore more respectful of the body of Gaia. The rise of Buddhist influence in the UU midst reflects a hunger for a more *mindful faith*, willing to be disciplined, fully present in the moment, and aware of the depths as well as the drama of being, and of UUs' compassionate connection with all sentient beings.

Feminist and liberation theologies call us to a more *prophetic faith*, a more risk-taking faith, daring to name what is broken, to challenge assumptions and to take actions requiring discomfort and sacrifice, that we might contribute more effectively to the repair and transformation of our world. They remind us that talking is not enough.

All of these newer emphases within the UU faith tradition call us to the disciplined embodiment of our values and commitments and the strengthening of those qualities that will help us to live them with integrity—to be more whole and to contribute to making the world more whole. This is more than a new spin on "salvation by character" and "service to humankind—onward and upward forever." It challenges UUs to incorporate a wholeness of being and contemporary ideas into the UU tradition's long-held commitments.

Every strand of the UU tradition holds up a mirror to our lives and to the society in which we live. Each brings both critique and constructive practice. Every strand has evolved in recent decades toward a more inclusive vision of wholeness and interconnectedness. Each brings a somewhat different perspective and body of wisdom to the circle of dialogue. As UUs grow more diverse, we are also growing toward more solid common ground.

Notes

1. James Luther Adams, "The Changing Reputation of Human Nature," revised reprint from *The Journal of Liberal Religion* (Autumn 1942 & Winter 1942): 23.
2. William Schulz, *Making the Manifesto: The Birth of Religious Humanism* (Boston: Skinner House, 2002), xix.
3. Suzuki, David, *The Sacred Balance: Rediscovering our Place in Nature* (Vancouver: Douglas & McIntyre, 1997), 191, 195-196.
4. Bernard Meland, quoted in Jerome A. Stone, *The Minimalist Vision of Transcendence: A Naturalist Philosophy of Religion* (New York: State University Press, 1992), 156.
5. Margot Adler, *Heretic's Heart: A Journey Through Spirit and Revolution* (Boston: Beacon Press, 1997), 288-289.
6. David Parke, "Theological Directions of Unitarian Universalism for the Next 25 Years," *The Unitarian Universalist Christian*, vol. 44, no. 3-4 (1989): 16.
7. Alice Blair Wesley, *Our Covenant: The 2000-01 Minns Lectures—The Lay and Liberal Doctrine of the Church: The Spirit and the Promise of our Covenant* (Chicago: Meadville-Lombard, 2002), 19.
8. See William R. Murry "Religious Humanism Yesterday, Today, and Tomorrow," *Religious Humanism*, vol. 34, no. 3 & 4 (2000): 74.
9. Sarah Oelberg, "Reasonable Religion," *HUUmanists News*, no. 1 (2004): 4.
10. Richard Erhardt, "Beating a Cold Still Corpse," *First Days Record*, (December 1997): 9.
11. James Casebolt and Tiffany Niekro, "Some UUs Are More UU Than U: Theological Self-descriptors Chosen by Unitarian Universalists," *Review of Religious Research* 46, no. 3 (2005): 235-242.
12. Ernest Cassa (ed.), *Universalism in America: A Documentary History of a Liberal Faith*, (Boston: Skinner House, 1971), 36-37.
13. *Singing the Living Tradition*, reading 537.

14. Alice Blair Wesley, "Time and Character in Unitarian Universalist Faith" *The Unitarian Universalist Christian* 44, no. 1 (Spring 1989): 46

15. Jerome Stone, "What Is Religious Naturalism?" *Religious Humanism*, vol. 35, nos. 1 & 2 (2001): 67.

16. David Robinson, *The Unitarians and the Universalists* (Westport, CT: Greenwood Press, 1985), 11.

17. James Luther Adams, "The Changing Reputation of Human Nature," a revised reprint from *The Journal of Liberal Religion* (Autumn 1942 & Winter 1942): 7.

18. Adams, "The Changing Reputation," 15.

19. Adams, "The Changing Reputation," 45-46.

20. Thandeka, "New Words for Life" in *Language of Reverence*, ed. Dean Grodzins (Chicago: Meadville Lombard Press, 2004), 75.

21. Carl Scovel, "Beyond Spirituality: The Berry Street Essay, 1994," in *Unitarian Universalism: Selected Essays* (Boston: UU Ministers Association, 1995), 8.

22. Nancy Arnold, "Our Faith as Unitarian Universalist," in *Unitarian Universalism: Selected Essays* (Boston: UU Ministers Association, 1996), 73.

23. Khoren Arisian "'The Promised Land': Humanism and Human Spirituality," *Religious Humanism*, vol. 34, nos. 1 & 2 (2000): 61.

24. Gary Kowalski, *Science and the Search for God* (New York: Lantern Books, 2003), 105.

25. Richard Gilbert, "Confessions of a Militant Mystic: Spirituality and Social Action—A Seamless Garment," in *Unitarian Universalism: Selected Essays* (Boston: UU Ministers Association, 1997), 13.

26. Gilbert, "Confessions," 8.

27. Lex Crane, "Rational Mysticism in UU Religion," in *Unitarian Universalism: Selected Essays* (Boston: UU Ministers Association, 1996), 31.

28. Scott Alexander, ed., *Everyday Spiritual Practice: Simple Pathways for Enriching Your Life* (Boston: Skinner House, 1999), 5.

29. Marilyn Sewell, *Wanting Wholeness, Being Broken* (Portland: Fuller Press, 1998), 113.

30. David Bumbaugh, "The Heart of a Faith for the Twenty-First Century," in *Unitarian Universalism: Selected Essays* (Boston: UU Ministers Association, 1994), 37.

31. Ken Wilber, *Sex, Ecology, Spirituality: The Spirit of Evolution* (Boston: Shambhala, 2000), 273.

32. Barbara Carlson, "An Awakened, Compassionate Life in Today's World," in *Unitarian Universalism: Selected Essays* (Boston: UU Ministers Association, 2001), 42.

33. John Cobb, "As Others See Us: Ecumenical Perspectives on Unitarian Universalism," *The Unitarian Universalist Christian*, (Winter 1987): 15.

34. See Wilber, pages 385-392.
35. Henry Nelson Wieman, *The Source of Human Good* (Carbondale, IL: Southern Illinois University, 1946), 105.
36. Jacques Derrida, *Deconstruction in a Nutshell: A Conversation with Jacques Derrida* (New York: Fordham University Press, 1997).
37. Daniel Adams, "Toward a Theological Understanding of Post-Modernism," *Cross Currents*, vol. 47, no. 4 (1997): 518-530. Also available online at www.aril.org/adams.htm.
38. Suzanne Meyer, "Claiming Our Prophetic Voice: The Modern Church in the Post-Modern World." Presented at the 2002 UUMA Convocation, Birmingham, Alabama. Available online at www.uuma.org/archives/Convocation/Modern%20Church%20Postmodern%20World%20Suzanne%20Meyer.html.
39. Leonard Sweet, *Faithquakes* (Nashville, TN: Abingdon Press, 1994).
40. Elizabeth Lesser and Huston Smith, "Are You Religious or Spiritual? Letters from the Heart," *Spirituality & Health* (Spring 2001). Available online at www.spiritualityhealth.com/newsh/items/article/item_2930.html.
41. Bumbaugh, "The Heart of a Faith," 36-38.
42. Charlotte Shivvers, "Moving Forward with Power Against Evil: Obstacles and Faith Center," in *Unitarian Universalism: Selected Essays* (Boston: UU Ministers Association, 1998), 55.
43. Phillip Hewett, "Reappropriating the Living Tradition," in *Unitarian Universalism: Selected Essays* (Boston: UU Ministers Association, 1997), 85, 89.

Worship: How Do We Celebrate?

According to former Starr King School for the Ministry president Robert C. Kimball, "Unitarian Universalists are people who like to go to church."[1] Worship—or for those who do not identify with that term, the Sunday morning program—is the most specifically religious way in which UU theologies manifest themselves in congregational life. While there are many kinds of events and activities in the lives of most UU congregations, it is the Sunday morning service that brings together the bulk of the people in UU communities. Consistent with the etymology of the word itself, through *worship* UUs ascribe worth; through congregational worship, we form a community around shared ascriptions of worth. The UUA can be seen as a joining together of worshipping congregations. In the course of our interviews and focus groups, many people suggested that worship is one means by which we find a common religious expression in the presence of diversity. Others, on the other hand, suggested that the content of the Sunday morning service is often the very thing that brings theological conflict to a head.

While this is not a study of worship, it was readily apparent to the Commissioners that worship, as an important source of both intra- and intercongregational unity and conflict, should be a major focus of this report. By surveying the member congregations, we hoped to see how the diversity of individual UU theologies shapes the worship life of our congregations. We also hoped to see just how comparable or diverse worship practices are across congregations.

Common Service Elements

The survey instrument contained items asking specifically about announcements, verbal joys and concerns, symbolic joys and concerns, and congregational readings. There was also an opportunity for free responses, allowing respondents to add other common service elements used in their congregations.

Announcements. Of all the worship-related practices about which the survey asked, none was more commonly reported than announcements: about 92 percent of congregations reported that announcements are made during their services. It was clear from the pattern of responses that for some congregations at least, announcements and how they should be made are a source of consternation. The respondent from one congregation wrote in large letters, "At last we got rid of announcements!" A few congregations made a point of stating that their announcements come before the lighting of their chalice, and therefore they do not consider them to be a part of the service. This is similar to a few other congregations that have attempted to banish other non-worshipful events (such as applause) while the chalice flame is lit. The orders of service enclosed by many respondents showed oral announcements appearing in nearly every conceivable place: at the very beginning of the service, after the introductory elements, and at the end.

Joys and Concerns. The majority of congregations take time in their services for the expression of joys and concerns, either verbally (86 percent) or symbolically (around 61 percent), such as through the lighting of candles. While we did not specifically track congregational size, it is clear that these practices (verbal expressions in particular) are much more common among small to mid-size congregations. In some congregations, the sharing of joys and concerns has been ritualized with the use of a song or a verbal liturgical element every week.

Readings. Exactly 75 percent of responding congregations reported the regular use of responsive or unison congregational readings in their services. Congregations were asked to rate the regularity of the use of readings or scriptures from several theological sources on a scale of 1 (never) to 10 (frequent). Specifically UU and literary sources typically received the highest ratings (with most congregations falling between 5 and 9), with several respondents reporting frequent use of secular poetry. These two were followed by humanist, Christian, and Jewish sources, in order of decreasing frequency around 4-5. Buddhist, pagan, and Native American writings received comparable ratings, with most congregations falling in the 2-5 range. The most consistent pattern in these results is the limited use of Hindu and Islamic writings, typically around 2 on the scale. Some congregations reported fairly uniform use of all but these two lowest categories. A distinct cluster of congregations, mostly small fellowships, gave high ratings to humanist writings in addition to the UU and literary sources, but rated all the rest as low. Another cluster rated only Christian and Jewish writings highly.

Chalice Lighting. There is no question that, in recent years, the lighting of a chalice at or near the beginning of a service has become an increasingly common event. In designing the form to be used in this survey, we intended for chalice lighting to be included on the checklist of service elements. However, through a proofreading error it was not included. Some congregational respondents wrote it in, and many others included sample orders of service that included the chalice lighting. These two categories added up to about 59 percent of responding congregations. However, chalice lightings are certainly more popular than this number would indicate. Since they were not specifically asked about it, some respondents may not have thought to include chalice lighting as a free response. Many congregations did not include sample orders of service that could be examined.

There is no question that, in recent years, the lighting of a chalice at or near the beginning of a service has become an increasingly common event.

When it came to extinguishing the chalice, only 18 percent of congregations reported this practice or sent sample orders of service listing it. We can safely conclude that someone, at some point, extinguishes the chalice; many congregations that light one, however, have not ritualized its extinguishing. Presumably in such congregations this is done as a matter of course during the benediction, closing words, or other service-concluding elements.

Sermon Reflection or Discussion. Less than 5 percent of congregations reported a time for response to the sermon as a part of the service. As with the chalice lighting, this is almost certainly an underestimate. In congregations where it is practiced, it may be so taken for granted that a respondent might not have thought to write it down.

On the other hand, several churches specifically reported eliminating this practice, at least as part of the service itself (such as by setting aside time for it during the refreshments following the service), or attempting to make it more of a sharing and less of an intellectual and often confrontational "talk-back."

Music

A total of 332 congregations (almost 90 percent of the total sample) reported using the most recent UUA hymnal, *Singing the Living Tradition*, either as their only hymnal (323) or with supplementation from another (9). Eight congregations reported that they use no hymnal, most explicitly stating that they do not sing in their services.

Children's Recessionals. One of the most common usages of a fixed hymn is as a children's recessional or children's benediction or simply for "singing the children out." A total of seventy-five congregations (about 20 percent of the total) reported using hymn 413 in *Singing the Living Tradition*, "Go Now in Peace," for this purpose; many of the congregations that simply reported singing this hymn may use it in this way as well. Only nineteen congregations reported using a song other than "Go Now In Peace" as a children's recessional.

The lyrics to "Go Now In Peace" printed in *Singing the Living Tradition* include the phrase, "May the love of God surround you." However, the song is often sung using the words "May the spirit of love surround you." Since many of the congregations that reported use of this song as a children's benediction did not send an order of service containing the lyrics used locally, there was no way to track this variation. However, the majority of congregations that *did* enclose orders of service use these alternative words rather than the ones in the hymnal.

Doxologies. Only about 23 percent (eighty-five) of responding congregations reported the use of a doxology. By far the most common song used was hymn 381 in *Singing the Living Tradition*, "From All That Dwell Below the Skies." Fifty-four congregations reported use of this song in some form, forty-seven as written in *Singing the Living Tradition*. Four congregations use adaptations of the original words, and three sing it in both English and Spanish.

Nine congregations reported the use of *Singing the Living Tradition* #123, "Spirit of Life," as a doxology. Six said they use a custom-written or unique song not appearing in *Singing the Living Tradition* or other recent UU hymnals.

General Hymns. If the use of a hymn as a children's recessional is eliminated, "Spirit of Life" is by far the most commonly sung UU song. Sixty-two congregations reported that this song, as written or with some adaptation, is used regularly in their services. In some cases it is used as an anthem, a closing song with the benediction, or a response to joys and concerns. No other song was reported as regularly used by more than six congregations. An outsider examining UU worship practices would almost certainly regard "Spirit of Life" as the standard UU anthem.

Anyone who served as a banner carrier at the 2002 General Assembly in Quebec City witnessed a graphic display of the place of this song in UU worship life. Prior to the opening ceremony, as the banner carriers were corralled in a waiting area, one of their number had a heart attack. As the paramedics arrived and began to care for this gentleman, the crowd began to sing "Spirit of Life" over and over again, very softly, and then to hum the

An outsider examining UU worship practices would almost certainly regard "Spirit of Life" as the standard UU anthem.

tune until the victim was removed from the room. To the bystanders, this song was the clearest imaginable expression of their support and a way to reduce their own anxieties. Nothing could more explicitly encapsulate the place that "Spirit of Life" has won in the hearts and minds of many UUs.

Special Services

The survey instrument gave respondents a list of special services and asked them to indicate which ones were held regularly in their congregation. This list included Holy Communion, Flower Communion/Flower Sunday, Bread Sunday, Christmas Eve, Passover Seder, Children's Sunday/Religious Education Sunday, and Water Communion. Respondents were also asked to list other special services held on a regular basis in their congregation, an opportunity they did not pass up.

A number of interesting and unique services were listed by responding congregations, but these are not the main interest of this study since we are looking for norms and commonalities. Table 1 in the statistical appendix gives more complete information regarding responses to this question.

If this sampling of congregations is in any way representative, it is clear that Norbert Čapek's flower ceremony, commonly referred to as the flower communion, has captured the collective UU imagination; almost 88 percent of congregations indicated that the flower ceremony is a regular part of their worship life. One congregation even mentioned a recent practice of incorporating the flower communion ritual format into memorial services for members who have died.

It is clear that Norbert Čapek's flower ceremony, commonly referred to as the flower communion, has captured the collective UU imagination.

Over 70 percent of congregations reported annual Christmas Eve services, children's or religious education services, and water ceremonies/communions. Passover seders were reported by about 35 percent of congregations. All other special theme services had frequencies of less than 20 percent.

Communion deserves some special attention. There was *not* a clear pattern, as might be expected, of Communion being maintained to a greater extent by New England churches. Nor was there an obvious correlation with historically Unitarian or Universalist congregations or with congregational size. Where Communion is held (in 64 congregations, which is about 17 percent), it is performed an average of 2.7 times per year. Five congregations reported performing Communion ten times or more per year; five others said it was held only every other year or "infrequently."

Of the services not explicitly listed on the form but reported using the free-response line, some variation on the All Souls ritual was most commonly listed (forty-four congregations). Of the thirty-three churches listing a specific Thanksgiving ritual, fifteen described it as a sort of harvest communion, usually incorporating cider and cornbread. Five others said that they perform a seder, like that detailed in Carl Seaburg's *The Communion Book*.[2]

At the bottom of the list, only one congregation reported using Soulful Sundown; in their free-response space at the end of the questionnaire, two congregations said they had abandoned this service because of lack of participation or interest. Soulful Sundown is an alternative worship format designed to appeal to youth and young adults that is frequently held in the evenings and centered around diverse kinds of music. If this experiential approach is not supported in UU congregations, what other shifts in worship practice might meet the perceived needs of youth and young adults?

Respondents were also asked to report on changes to their service selections in the last ten years. The responses show a clear pattern of adding more ritualized services. The four special services listed as the most frequent above (flower communion, water communion, Christmas Eve, and Passover) were also the most commonly listed new additions. The Passover seder was also the most commonly eliminated, however. A number of other novel service forms were reported by only one congregation; some of these may spread and become common in the future. Table 2 in the statistical appendix gives more detailed results for this question.

Covenants and Affirmations

An examination of the statements of covenant and affirmation used in UU congregations shows a very distinct pattern of variations on a few basic themes. Of the 370 congregations submitting surveys, 203 (about 55 percent) reported that they do not use any specific covenant or affirmation in their worship on a regular basis. For a precise breakdown of the covenants used regularly by 45 percent of the responding congregations, see Table 3 in the worship survey appendix.

A text specific to the congregation, such as its mission statement, is used as a covenant or affirmation by forty-nine congregations. With the exception of one congregation that uses the Winchester Profession, all other congregations reported using a text that is in, or is based on a text in, the most commonly used hymnal.

The current UUA hymnal, *Singing the Living Tradition*, includes five readings explicitly identified as covenants. Of these, the ones attributed to J. Griswold Williams (471), Charles Gordon Ames (472), and James Vila Blake (473) have shown themselves to be popular targets for revision. In reality, the versions of these covenants in *Singing the Living Tradition* are themselves revisions. In some cases the variations currently used in some congregations are more similar to the originals than the hymnal versions are.

According to the section "Notes on Hymns, Tunes, and Readings" in *Hymns for the Celebration of Life*,[3] the Williams covenant was originally entitled "A Covenant for Free Worship." L. Griswold Williams was a Universalist minister and compiler of the original source of this covenant, *Antiphonal Readings for Free Worship*, which was published in 1933. James Vila Blake was a Unitarian minister. The covenant attributed to him was adopted in 1894 by the Unitarian church in Evanston, Illinois, during Blake's tenure in its pulpit. Charles Gordon Ames, who began his ministry as a Free Baptist missionary, composed the covenant bearing his name for the use of the Spring Garden Unitarian Society in Philadelphia. His twenty years of ministry to the Church of the Disciples (Unitarian) in Boston in the early 1900s may explain the popularity of his covenant in New England.

The Williams and Blake covenants are very similar in their original versions. Some congregational covenants represent amalgams or blendings of the two to the point that it is difficult to determine which was the foundational text. Here are the texts as printed in *Singing the Living Tradition*:

The Williams covenant:
Love is the doctrine of this church,
The quest for truth is its sacrament,
And service is its prayer.
To dwell together in peace,
To seek knowledge in freedom,
To serve human need,
To the end that all souls shall grow
　　into harmony with the Divine—
Thus do we covenant with each
　　other and with God.

The Blake covenant:
Love is the spirit of this church,
　　and service is its law.
This is our great covenant:
To dwell together in peace,
To seek the truth in love,
And to help one another.

A total of forty-two congregations reported regular use of the Williams covenant, twenty-seven of them with some adaptation. The most common adaptations of the Williams covenant, in decreasing order of frequency, were:

- dropping or rephrasing "with God" in the covenant language at the end (27)
- replacing "human need," most commonly with "humankind in fellowship" or "humanity in fellowship" (21)
- completely dropping the language referring to "growing into harmony" (11)
- dropping or rewording the reference to "the Divine" (10)
- using possessive "our" instead of "its" in the opening lines (5)
- dropping "with each other" from the covenant language at the end (5)
- replacing the word "doctrine" with "spirit" (5)

- replacing "church" in the opening line (4)
- dropping the use of "is" in the opening lines (3)
- dropping all covenant language at the end (3)

The phrase "mankind in fellowship" in the *Hymns for the Celebration of Life* (1964) version was replaced with "human need" in *Singing the Living Tradition* to make the text more gender-neutral. Many congregational variations instead use the phrase "humankind in fellowship," a more neutral but less extreme change. Perhaps these versions predate the publication of the version in *Singing the Living Tradition*.

Of the forty-one congregations reporting regular use of the Blake covenant, nineteen adapted it in some way. Common variations on the Blake covenant included:

- replacing the word "church" with a word more in keeping with the nature or name of the congregation, such as "fellowship"
- adding the word "is" in the phrase "and service its law," a change that increases the parallel construction with the opening line
- replacing of the word "law" with a word carrying less doctrinaire implications

Nine congregations reported covenants that are amalgamations of lines from both the Williams and Blake covenants. In several of these variations, the word "covenant" is replaced with "aspiration" with an accompanying change of verb form to reflect a hope for the future (or perhaps a continuity into the future) rather than just a current state of affairs.

Only four congregations reported use of the Ames covenant. In every case it had been adapted from the text in *Singing the Living Tradition*.

The Ames covenant:
In the freedom of truth,
And the spirit of Jesus,
We unite for the worship of God
And the service of all.

The reported adaptations appear to be altering the text in two opposing directions. Some make it less Christian by replacing "Jesus" with "Love," while others make it more explicitly Christian by adding "Christ" to the second line. Of those that maintain the original reference to Jesus, the common alteration is the replacement of "freedom" with "love."

Rites of Passage

Unitarian Universalists have developed a variety of rites of passage for members and nonmembers of their congregations. The list is probably familiar: namings, dedications, welcomings (for adopted children), and christenings; weddings, holy unions, rededications of vows, and ceremonies of divorce; funerals, memorials, cremations, and burials; and of course, ordinations and installations of clergy. Frequently these ceremonies are crafted for the particular occasion both in text and structure. Unitarian Universalists have been doing this for years. All of these ceremonies serve to strengthen the bonds within families and between individuals and their spiritual communities.

Unitarian Universalists have developed a variety of rites of passage to strengthen the bonds within families and between individuals and their spiritual communities.

Some congregations have rituals for the induction of new members, newly elected trustees, committee chairs, deacons, and members of pastoral care teams. These all allow the congregation to view those taking on particular tasks so that they will know whom to approach for particular requests, and they serve as all or part of a covenanting process with the other members of the congregation.

What is relatively new and exciting is the development of bridging ceremonies for our youth as they become young adults. The first time such a ceremony occurred at the continental level was at the 1995 General Assembly. They occur on the district and congregational levels as well. Bridging ceremonies are designed to avoid the so-called "cliff"—the point at which our youth often find themselves when they have aged out of Young Religious Unitarian Universalists and before they go out into the world of work or college. It can seem to them that there is nothing in their congregation's environment specifically for them. This is of course a critical time because it may be when we begin to lose them.

While rites of passage were not explicitly listed on the worship survey questionnaire, some were listed in the free responses of many congregations (see Table 3 in the statistical appendix). These included new member ceremonies, child dedications, and coming of age services. Of the rites of passage mentioned in the preceding paragraphs, these three are most commonly performed during Sunday morning services. Most of the others are stand-alone events or are incorporated into other special occasions.

Concluding Reflections

The worship survey undertaken by the Commission indicated that of the responding congregations, 92 percent had announcements and 88 percent celebrated the flower ceremony. The most regularly used song was "Spirit of Life"; and the most common sources for readings were literary and Unitarian Universalist in origin.

These four observations from the survey data might seem a satisfying acknowledgment of the unity in our theological diversity. Announcements are a way of sharing interests and concerns about congregational and community life. The flower ceremony is a way in which each person present can both give and receive. The hymn "Spirit of Life" has a mellow, soothing quality, reaffirming our desire to be good, justice-making folk. The use of literary and Unitarian Universalist sources for our readings suggests that we value the spiritual resources offered by the secular world outside our faith and that we affirm the values of our coreligionists. What could be worrisome about this picture? Obviously, the survey has reported many other points of agreement among UUs.

In a presentation entitled "The Risky Venture of Worship," Professor Robin W. Lovin of the Perkins School of Theology at Southern Methodist University noted that

> Most people in American mainstream Protestant congregations do not come to church predisposed to worship. . . . The basic experience of worship, in which we offer something and are transformed by what happens in the offering—that basic experience . . . is foreign. Indeed they have been prepared to expect something quite the opposite. The basic model for what we do together in our affluent, consumer-oriented society is not *offering*, but *acquisition*. . . . It's as if the event has to reassure us that in the end, it's all really about us and who we are.[4]

Lovin further notes that we are now becoming accustomed to an entertainment model and asks, "What could be farther from the point of real worship than a preacher and a congregation whose experience is primarily being satisfied with each other's company?"

Although Lovin is not speaking of UUs, his cautions are well taken. Worship services are the most obvious opportunity for members of a congregation to be with each other regularly. Because UU theological diversity militates against any generalized sense that UUs are offering themselves to God in worship, we have to ask, just what are UUs doing at their services?

If members think they are sharing, they might heed another of Lovin's cautions: "What's important to people who are 'sharing' . . . is that everybody else receive what is shared and nobody challenges or changes it." For worship to be what it can be, "you have to do things that break the cultural assumption that when we give, what we are doing is 'sharing' in expectation of recognition and affirmation."

Lovin's comment may help explain why some UUs are uncomfortable with the announcements so frequently found in their worship. They are a form of sharing to which there can be no authentic response in the moment.

Those who sing "Spirit of Life" can also see that the words are basically about them: The Spirit is here to help us be who we want to be. Even the flower ceremony, the heartfelt and heartbreaking gift of Norbert Čapek in the concentration camp, has in effect become a sharing, so that its beauty and power can be reduced to a pleasant festivity.

No major religious tradition lacks the element of offering in worship. And that offering is most importantly not the offering of material goods but of the congregant or worshipper. If UUs do not somehow begin to reclaim the experience of offering in worship, they may well find that their theological diversity and differing interests will slowly move them further and further apart. If, however, we begin to engage the issue now in adult classes, in the religious education of children and youth, and from the pulpit, we have a chance to employ the enormous richness of our theological diversity in the service of making worship a place to learn how to be more authentic and generous in our personal and public relations and commitments.

It is perhaps not a *language* of reverence that is needed, so much as a *practice* of reverence. It is not whether we call upon the Spirit of Life or God/Goddess and see that energy operative in our lives but what *we offer to life*. It is not enough to want readings or sermons to inspire us; we have to be *willing* to be inspired, even if it might mean we have to rethink things and possibly do things differently. This doesn't require a particular theology or theistic thinking. It requires an attitude shift from self-cherishing to a sense of openness and interdependence in our worship. That does not mean a relinquishing of self-value or a denial of self-worth, just a shift in perspective. And that shift will slowly but surely grow beauty in our common life and reinvigorate our efforts toward the justice-making we yearn for.

It is perhaps not a language of reverence that is needed, so much as a practice of reverence.

Notes

1. Personal communication.
2. Carl Seaburg, ed., *The Communion Book* (Boston: Unitarian Universalist Ministers Association, 1993).
3. *Hymns for the Celebration of Life* (Boston: Unitarian Universalist Association, 1964).
4. This and the following Lovin quotes from the 2004 James Luther Adams Lecture.

Justice Making: How Shall We Serve?

Am I my brother's or sister's keeper? The question is old; the controversy is current. What is the mission of Unitarian Universalists, individually and collectively? What ethical imperatives grow from UU values and worldviews? Should UU congregations be a presence in the community and if so, how? Can a congregation as a whole take a public stand on a controversial issue? Should the Unitarian Universalist Association do so? Would doing so violate the personal convictions of one or more members, and is this inconsistent with the Purposes and Principles of the congregations and Association? Should members be urged to personal involvement in issues and causes rather than have the corporate entity of a congregation involved? How should the rights of both the majority and minority be balanced? How effective are the Study-Action Issues so extensively discussed at General Assembly in any given year? And what comes of the Actions of Immediate Witness so hotly debated, apart from becoming a record to which UUA leaders can point in subsequent years? The questions are endless.

On the COA theology questionnaire of 2004, four broad mission affirmations received consistent ratings as highly important. They are listed here with a brief commentary on each.

We challenge ourselves and our world to look for options other than violence to resolve differences. This statement received the highest ranking, perhaps due in part to current concerns, especially the attacks in the United

States on September 11, 2001; events in Afghanistan; and the war in Iraq.

We need to challenge ourselves and our world to build bridges of understanding and respect across differences. UU feminist theologian Sharon Welch explains,

> The disuniting of America has two strands: ambiguity and difference. . . . In order to understand [them and to live with them], we need a sense of self and community fluid enough to learn from and with differences and mistakes. What bothers me about the calls for common ground is that this very concept of community is predicated on denying what I see as the richness of community, a richness created as much by difference and surprise as by similarity and affirmation.[1]

We are committed to the work of dismantling prejudice, racism, and all types of oppression. Rev. Richard Gilbert offers a kind of caveat:

> For some time now I have had a "lovers' quarrel" with our movement. When I was a graduate student . . . a fellow student, a Catholic Worker priest, asked me point-blank, "How can your denomination, middle class as it is, critique the system that has so favored it?" It was a disturbing question. I have been troubled by his implied accusation ever since. There is a temptation among us to be complacent. . . . By and large we benefit from the status quo. . . . How, then, can we exhibit the prophetic zeal to envision what might and ought to be, much less be in the vanguard of those who seek to bring that vision to reality? This relative complacency is as much a spiritual as a social problem.[2]

We challenge ourselves to question values (such as consumerism and conformity) permeating our society. Voices challenging UUs to question society's assumptions are coming from many strands of their tradition, including from Canadian minister and scholar Phillip Hewett:

> Our role, I submit, is to draw from our living tradition and to prophecy. . . . [There are] people who are saying . . . that we will not get very far into the next millennium unless we change our ways very drastically. I believe them. I believe also that such a change presents an almost insuperable challenge. It calls for what in the Hebrew tradition was called teshuvah—a dramatic and drastic turning from one path to another. Our role is nothing less than to promote such a *teshuvah*.[3]

Right relationship with the natural world means cooperating and protecting, not controlling. The preceding four issues lead to a fifth concern, which ranks highly among UUs today, concern for the environment. The "interconnected web" metaphor has only been central for our movement for just over twenty years, yet it has become an important component of our self-understanding. Articulated in the Seventh Principle Project and the Green Sanctuary movement, this was the focus of the 2004 General Assembly study/action resolution.

Among the results of a 1966 study, as reported by Robert Tapp in his 1973 book *Religion Among the Unitarian Universalists*, social action was ranked fifth in importance by respondents who asked about institutional emphases for the church. Specific areas for church action were, in descending order, racial integration, juvenile delinquency, poverty, mental illness, drug addiction, sexual morality, alcoholism, organized crime, and gambling. Tapp used the label *traditionals* for people who described themselves as Christians and wanted their denomination to move toward Christianity. *Posttraditionals* were described as moving away from Christian roots. While both groups were concerned about juvenile delinquency, poverty, racial integration, and mental illness, traditionals were more concerned with sexual morality than posttraditionals were. According to Tapp, "The posttraditionals were much more ready to regard integration and poverty as very important, and much less ready to so regard gambling, sexual morality, or alcoholism. . . . The posttraditionals . . . are more concerned with areas of social ethics and less with . . . personal ethics."[4] The topics and results were a clear picture of the concerns and values of the 1960s.

How should a congregation address controversial issues? Not surprisingly, Tapp found that the first choice was discussion meetings, followed by sermons, public stands by a minister, participation in demonstrations by members, public stands by congregation, participation in demonstrations by minister, and public stands by a committee. The 1960s were a time of upheaval within both the newly formed UUA and the United States at large.

The issues have changed, but passionate advocacy based on deeply held religious values continues to impel UUs into active engagement with their world. The approach to addressing issues still reflects a pattern of becoming informed, developing a position, and then doing something about the area of concern. The role of a minister in public advocacy remains a sensitive issue. In all probability, this will continue to be the case. Unitarian Universalists are not alone in the related dilemmas, but this is scarcely comforting.

The list of famous Unitarians and Universalists is replete with names of change agents in their time, people who felt empowered by their religious values to go out and do their best to improve the lives of others. In many cases, they and their work were derided by their contemporaries, including their coreligionists. There is arguably more respect currently for Theodore Parker, Susan B. Anthony, Benjamin Rush, and Clara Barton than they

Passionate advocacy based on deeply held religious values continues to impel UUs into active engagement with their world.

received during their lifetimes. To the extent that they were able to build a constituency within and, more importantly, beyond their religious communities, their work outlasted their lives, particularly in the cases of Barton (American Red Cross) and Anthony (women's suffrage).

Social action was institutionalized with the creation of the Universalist and Unitarian service committees. These agencies merged in 1963 into the Unitarian Universalist Service Committee (UUSC), an associate member of the UUA, which currently operates programs both domestically and internationally. Historically, the Universalist Service Committee included opportunities for volunteers to work domestically (as at the Jordan Neighborhood House in Suffolk, Virginia) and internationally (as at Jugendwerk Druhwald in Germany). The Unitarian Service Committee was formed to aid refugees from Spain during the Spanish Civil War in the late 1930s and subsequently people displaced by World War II. A number of current UUs express the concern that the volunteer component of the UUSC could be better organized. It recently created the Just Works program in order to address perceived deficits in such programming. In the late twentieth century and early twenty-first century, most volunteer openings are in fundraising with congregations and districts in support of advocacy programs, rather than hands-on opportunities for people with skills, time, and a desire to share them through work within the formal context of Unitarian Universalism and from a deep sense of commitment to the highest values they associate with their faith. This would, optimally, be a both/and situation.

Congregations have organized to meet needs in their local communities, often spinning off these projects into community-supported organizations with participation by others sharing their concerns. For example, in the name of the church or fellowship, congregation members have created or supported soup kitchens, refugee resettlement projects, inner-city school tutoring, projects to build school playgrounds, and similar programs to meet identified local needs. Church committees have initiated or supported local, state, and national legislation. The first, second, and seventh Principles of the Unitarian Universalist Association encourage involvement of people and congregations in their world, and many take this very seriously. As Englishman Roger Housden observes in *Sacred America*, "An almost quasi-religious fervor for volunteerism has long been ingrained in the mythos of this country [the United States]."[5] The French observer Alexis de Tocqueville made a similar comment in his 1831 book *Democracy in America*. Unitarian Universalists have long participated in the volunteer culture, as illustrated in responses to questions asked of congregations, focus groups, and individuals by members of the Commission on Appraisal.

Ministry in the Community

Over time, such activities as those described above have been called social action or social service projects or programs. Increasingly, congregations are calling them *ministries*, a change in both term and concept. Historically, projects have tended to be short lived—"one-shots," as it were—presumably to meet the needs or desires of contemporary people who are less willing to enter into long-term commitments than some of their predecessors. Many observers have commented on the short attention spans of Americans. Projects are often self-limiting, identified with the vision and commitment of the individuals who participate. As with many things in the Unitarian Universalist world, individuals' interests and desires often guide what happens.

Conceptually, the word *ministry* connotes an institutional commitment, an outreach in the name of the church or fellowship rather than of a committee or other subgroup. Individual participants may come or go, but the ministry is ongoing, enjoying the support and official sanction of the congregation and its leadership, both clerical and lay.

Pathways Church, the start-up Unitarian Universalist congregation in Northeast Tarrant County, Texas, provides a good illustration of the broadened view of ministry. The congregation describes itself as "an inclusive, hope-centered church where every member has a ministry." Under "Core Vision," its website lists seven statements about what "we are challenged to become in the future." Fourth in this list is, "We envision helping all our people—children and youth as well as adults—to find opportunities for ways of making a difference in the world through some ministry either within or outside the church. Our goal is that every member have a ministry of some kind."

For many years, Unitarian Universalists have shied away from traditional language, including ministry in a broader sense than the services provided by the minister of a particular congregation. One result is self-marginalization within the general community; the congregation may fall beneath the radar of that wider community, becoming irrelevant—not so much excluded because of theological issues as ignored.

One example of a relatively new ministry in a number of UU churches, as in other faith communities, is parish nursing. Donald Skinner cites examples in the March/April 2004 issue of *UU World*. He says that "typically, the program consists of a nurse who volunteers to minister to the physical needs of congregants."[6] This is a form of ministry to congregants—to the church community. When members of the Commission on Appraisal asked participants in focus groups, at hearings, and on questionnaires what it is that keeps them within their congregations, a common answer was "a sense of community," although it is unclear what the commonalities of this community are. A successful community is said to adapt

For many years, Unitarian Universalists have shied away from traditional language. One result is self-marginalization within the general community; the congregation may fall beneath the radar of that wider community, not so much excluded as ignored.

to and serve the needs of its members. In these times of reduced health coverage, high medical and insurance expenses, and greater distances to health care providers, churches and fellowships with the human resources are making the appropriate adaptations to honor and serve the interdependence of members of their communities. Ministry can and should include outreach within and beyond the immediate congregation, and this ministry can be provided by people other than ordained ministers. The organizers of Pathways Church, for example, have wisely recognized this.

International Connections

The Commissioners would be remiss if they did not mention collaborative and supportive activities between UU congregations and coreligionists abroad. Theological differences are evident in the statements of belief among these groups, but the similarities and histories are enough to forge a bond. Relationships exist between individual congregations in North America and congregations and religious institutions abroad. A significant number of these arrangements work through the Partner Church Council, especially in Romania (Transylvania), Hungary, the Czech Republic, and increasingly, India and the Philippines. The International Council of Unitarians and Universalists and the International Association for Religious Freedom also provide opportunities for interaction and cooperation with co-religionists and allies in these and other countries.

Several congregations operate or support non–Unitarian Universalist projects in South America and Africa. A significant characteristic in the philosophical and religious underpinnings of these activities is that they focus on mutuality, not conversion, which distinguishes them from work done by many other religious groups. There is a charitable component, especially where the churches have existed under—and survived—hostile governments in their countries. At the same time, groups stress the reciprocal nature of the partnerships.

Writing about outreach and generosity, Rev. Ruth Ellen Gibson of First Universalist Church in Denver observed, "The Partner Church work is part of our mission. . . . Each year, there is a special collection for our partner church work. . . . We operate on the idea that transforming our community is part of the work of the church, and that generosity will be motivated differently for different people. . . . Nearly everyone feels better about their church, and happier to pledge to the church, as they see the church doing good work in the world."

Does UUs' work for justice and compassion in the world unite them? Given that at least four of the UU Principles have social action implications, it would seem so. The UU faith has offered a supportive and meaningful home to many people who have made a difference in the world. Yet most of the significant historical actions for change referred to earlier are associated with prophetic individuals rather than communities, let alone the Association as a whole. The General Assembly passes resolutions; the challenge is for congregations to act on them.

Community action has the power to unite members of a congregation, and often it has; it has also at times alienated individuals and split congregations. Because of UUs' commitment to freedom of conscience, different individuals or groups within UU ranks may have different ideas about how to implement the Principles supporting human worth, social justice, and environmental responsibility. Persistent dialogue within congregations is crucial in attempting to agree on what congregation-wide actions or stands can be appropriately adopted. While some congregations may conclude no such united action is possible, persisting with dialogue usually allows a congregation to find one or more missions or ministries for social change that its members can widely embrace. Few things strengthen a community so much as a clear sense of relevant prophetic mission.

What Unitarian Universalists consider relevant has shifted significantly since the 1967 *Report of the Committee on Goals*. Only one of the areas of concern in that survey, racism, is still a major one for UU congregations. Other current areas of concern named at the beginning of this chapter took different form in earlier decades. A prime example of shifting perspectives is that thirty-seven years ago, 88 percent of UUs surveyed felt that homosexuality should be discouraged, if not by law (8 percent) then by education (80 percent).[7] Now the Welcoming Congregation program is an important part of the collective identity in a large number of UU churches.

How UUs understand social responsibility has shifted as well. UUs even approach antiracism work, a continuing theme, differently. Unitarian Universalism is still interested in social transformation, but UUs no longer focus almost exclusively outside themselves to change others; with deepened humility, UUs examine themselves and their own contributions to the patterns of society as well. Thus, concern for juvenile delinquency and gambling has given way to sexism and racism audits, Welcoming Congregation trainings, Green Sanctuary projects, voluntary simplicity circles, and Alternatives to Violence trainings. Perhaps the contemporary challenge is to balance such honest reflection with prophetic action, in the words of one UU Principles statement: "to confront powers and structures of evil with justice, compassion, and the transforming power of love."

UU theology is incomplete unless it is manifest in personal and institutional prophetic witness, and UU social action is inadequate unless it is congruent with the church's religious history and principles. Therefore, the Commission on Appraisal encourages Unitarian Universalists, both as individuals and communities, to be intentional about grounding social action in disciplined ethical study and rigorous theological reflection, and in honest, caring, and persistent dialogue with one another and with those outside UU ranks. Such study, reflection, and dialogue and the mindful action that follows are important forms of UU spiritual practice.

Clearly, one source of unity amid UUs' diversity is their dedication to making their theology manifest in the larger world. UUs are summoned to become theologically informed prophetic servants, wherever they are planted. Their ways of action will differ, but UUs' commitment is universal and unbending. In the Unitarian Universalist way of being and doing religion, faith and ethics are unified.

Living in a time when both human welfare and the natural world are threatened in a multitude of ways, is the UU role nothing less than to promote a *teshuvah*—"a dramatic and drastic turning from one path to another"? If UUs find common ground in such a challenge for their time, what possibilities and actions are they called to embrace in service to this vision?

Notes

1. Sharon Welsh, *Sweet Dreams in America: Making Ethics and Spirituality Work* (Portland: Fuller Press, 1999), 61-62.
2. Richard S. Gilbert, *The Prophetic Imperative*, rev. edition (Boston: Skinner House Press, 2001), 20.
3. Phillip Hewett, "Reappropriating the Living Tradition," in *Unitarian Universalism: Selected Essays* (Boston: UU Ministers Association, 1997), 94.
4. Robert B. Tapp, *Religion among the Unitarian Universalists: Converts in the Stepfathers' House* (New York: Seminar Press, 1973), 21.
5. Roger Housden, *Sacred America: The Emerging Spirit of the People* (New York: Simon & Schuster, 1999), 60.
6. Donald E. Skinner, "Healthier Congregations Through Parish Nursing," *UUWorld* (March/April 2004), 16.
7. Gilbert, *The Prophetic Imperative*, p. 32.

Community: How Do We Come Together?

Each church member brings a different understanding of the UU faith into his or her religious community; each brings a different hope for how to experience religious and spiritual life. One theology cannot fit every kind of Unitarian Universalist today. Within the UU religious movement, which embraces a spirit of questioning and daring, permeates a strong and steady fear of "the other." It is not easy to have that which we hold dear threatened by "the other" either.

Paul Rasor, director of the Social Witness Program at the Quaker study center Pendle Hill, asserts,

> Liberals want to create a strong and inclusive community but we often want to do it without giving up anything, without letting down the barriers we erect around ourselves in the name of individual autonomy.[1]

The reality is that while UUs do hold these ideals, we live in messy worlds where living our faith does not come easily. Our idealism encourages us to make ourselves accountable to high (and diverse) authorities. Feeling disappointed with shallow outcomes, we take stock. Although our best intentions often fall short, we can tell where we stand on the continuum of embodied faith.

When listening to people across the continent, the Commission found that theologically, as diverse as UUs are, what unifies us far outweighs

As diverse as UUs are, what unifies us far outweighs what divides us.

what divides us. We are a community of faith given to engagement with our world, using the power of the institution to work for justice and freedom—religious or otherwise. The core of UU faith embraces our theological similarities and differences.

Among the obvious indicators of theology made manifest are the UU religious education programs, calls to social action, diverse worship practices, habits of stewardship, and acts of hospitality. Less obvious indicators include informational pamphlets, orders of service, hymnals, the Wayside Pulpit, celebrations such as Divali (the Hindu Festival of Lights) or El Día de los Muertos (the Mexican Day of the Dead), the Green Sanctuary initiative (helping UUs walk an environmentally oriented religious path), youth chaplaincy training programs and chaplaincy opportunities, Soulful Sundown, covenant groups, and designated fellowship spaces.

These are all well and good, but UUs can stretch and challenge themselves and make these indicators stronger and sounder yet. Congregations can do the audits and ask whether UU pamphlets are available in a language or languages other than English. We can ask ourselves if our orders of service are user-friendly, especially to newcomers; whether our signage is relatively easy for all visitors to understand; if our membership guidelines make provisions for the financially fragile; if we are paying close enough attention to language, culture, identity, and physical ability.

Some indicators are even more difficult to discern. We must scrutinize all UU activities for any signs of oppression or discrimination; offer worship spaces that are welcoming to members and visitors with differing physical abilities; ensure that the fellowship hour following Sunday worship serves exclusively as social time; and avoid using jargon in the company of outsiders. It also includes the practice of good manners, such as not asking people what they are doing visiting a particular congregation; and sensitivity to religious practices that might seem foreign, particularly on unfamiliar holy days.

Indicators such as these are key for a strong sense of community, one that withstands a high degree of theological diversity. Many UUs told us that community is the bedrock of their faith. Over and over, attendees at our hearings and workshops described community as the cradle for the diversity within our unity.

How should UUs build a strong foundation of community? We build it brick by brick, step by step, with all of the sensitivity that we can muster. We build it knowing that we will make mistakes along the way. We also build it knowing that it will not be perfect.

Embracing community is a choice, an offering of heart and mind. Part of community is belonging to a group of people who strive to promote and sustain a healthy part of the individual and collective self. In community, we are offered opportunities to learn who we are; to recognize the permeable ways in which leadership is transmitted; and to be grateful for each other, for those on whose shoulders we stand, and for those who will in turn stand on our shoulders.

Hospitality

Participating in foundation-building helps UU congregations embrace the unity inherent in our diversity. A prophetic challenge is to be welcoming of "the other"—the idea, belief, or person who is a stranger to us—even when, or especially when, we do not wish to do so. We will be powerful in expressing our unity within our congregations when individuals can embrace the person whose expression and practice of faith differs from theirs. Are we ready for the challenge?

We will be powerful in expressing our unity within our congregations when individuals can embrace the person whose expression and practice of faith differs from theirs.

The challenge is a moral one that speaks directly to hospitality. UU congregations will not be as welcoming as they might be until we understand that hospitality is not an option but a necessity. *Webster's Dictionary* defines *hospitality* as "the act, practice, or quality of receiving and entertaining strangers or guests in a friendly and generous way."[2]

Meeting the challenge requires tolerating a certain amount of discomfort; in fact, it is not always safe. But life is transformed when we see the stranger as a potential friend. Many of our dearest friends were, in fact, strangers to us at one point.

Why should UUs take the time and make the effort to focus on hospitality? For one thing, all faith traditions share universal ideas about being welcoming. Hospitality is a religious practice, one that allows us to open our hearts to strangers, especially marginalized persons whom we could easily ignore. Our whole beings are stretched when we create and develop new ways of creating community.

The UUA has a tool that helps congregations assess where they fit on the "hospitality continuum." It is a part of a large program called The Uncommon Denomination. The following quote from one of the implementers of this survey, describing her church, speaks volumes:

> We had greeters at the doors, a welcome table for visitors, name tags, packets we mailed to people, and lots of activities for adults and children. Extroverts can pretty easily find their way into our community. But when we heard from two different visitors that no one talked to them when they came, we realized that we weren't as friendly as we thought. It's no comfort to know from visiting other UU churches that we're not alone in finding this a challenge.[3]

Engaging in hospitality takes courage. It requires us to make room for all voices to be heard and respected, especially those that might be disconcerting. And it requires being objective and ensuring that personal agendas do not sit at the bargaining table.

Embracing hospitality takes even more courage than simply engaging in it. When conflicts arise, we must commit ourselves to keeping an open mind, being willing to listen, and being willing to change our minds. Hosea Ballou, the father of modern Universalism, said, "If we agree in love, no disagreement can do us any harm. If we do not agree in love, no other agreement can do us any good."[4] These few words say much about a Unitarian Universalist understanding of faith-based conflict resolution.

In today's climate of transition, with its new needs and new possibilities, UUs are confronted with concomitant issues of culture, hospitality, and conflict avoidance. Theologian Howard Thurman spoke to this challenge, saying, "If I know what I ought to do in a given situation, if I see the action that I should take in order to be true to the deepest thing in me, if I look steadily in the eye and see not, the light that is in me becomes darkness."[5]

Conflict is a significant part of daily life. It should do nothing less than create an environment of challenge to move congregations forward toward hospitality. Moreover, conflict can lead to growth, new understandings, and deeper relationships. It can offer new perspectives and fresh ideas for moving forward.

These fresh ideas originate from the heart of hospitality. It is important to know a community's culture. Fresh ideas do not grow in a vacuum. In fostering a culture of hospitality, UUs should ask questions such as "Who are the theological policy makers in this congregation?" and "How are the grass roots within this community nurtured?" Being open to the responses strengthens the conversation as well as the community. The hospitality of hand and heart can help us live our faith together.

The practice of hospitality will not transform our congregations if it is viewed as only one more program in a series designed to strengthen UU houses of worship. The reality is that the majority of congregations must, at a fundamental level, come to feel that hospitality is a core part of our responsibility as authentic Unitarian Universalists. They must also come to share a vision of the congregation as a truly welcoming place. Positive outcomes may then result in increased enthusiasm for the congregation and growth in membership.

Hospitality takes people beyond their personal boundaries. It demands reaching out past discomfort as though the empty seat next to yours in the pew belongs to the stranger. We underestimate the power of a greeting or other sharing during the service whether the other is known to us, or not. Hospitality is far more than "hello." It is far more than receiving news in the sharing of joys and concerns. It is that tap on the seat next to yours that effectively says "Welcome, dear stranger. This seat belongs to you."

A core feature of religious freedom is the ability to be hospitable. Sister Joan Chittister asserts that "hospitality is the way we come out of ourselves. It is the first step toward dismantling the barriers of the world."[6] People interviewed by the Commission spoke of hospitality as the expression of welcome that we extend to each other, to friends, and to strangers. It starts from within our hearts. It is a reciprocal action.

When we recognize and welcome "the other," not only in our midst but also within ourselves, true hospitality is at work. Each is guest and each is host, bringing the best of our understanding to the depth of our faith. Hospitality is also a tool that we can use to help us form that solid base of unity within our diversity. In a global sense, hospitality is the practice of being welcoming.

Hospitality is a tool we can use to help us form that solid base of unity within our diversity.

Unitarian Universalists enjoy a relatively generous and safe environment in which to consider and reflect diverse expressions of our respective understandings of religion and Unitarian Universalism. Our own forebears were "the other," strangers in their environments.

The notion of being inclusive and reflecting our shared values is compelling. It is easy to worship with like-minded people who share our religious experience and sensibilities, but it is difficult to worship with those whose religious journeys take them along paths that are very different from ours.

The UUA offers many books, pamphlets, and other resources that can support hospitality efforts, such as *The Unitarian Universalist Pocket Guide*; *100 Questions That Non-Members Ask about Unitarian Universalism*; *Welcome to Unitarian Universalism: A Community of Truth, Service, Holiness and Love*; and *Building Your Own Theology*.

The importance of hospitality became clear to the Commission when we held four days of meetings at Glastonbury Abbey in Hingham, Massachusetts. The radical hospitality of the brothers created an environment within which we felt safe to deal with emotionally charged and potentially contentious issues and showed us that Unitarian Universalists could benefit from this approach to our fellow human beings. Benedictines describe hospitality as that which "enables you to joyfully make room for another inside your open heart."

If we truly honor our UU Principles, we cannot simply fight for freedom of religion "out there" without fighting for it "in here." Theological apartheid has no place in the practice of hospitality and religion. Theologian Howard Thurman reminds us that two kinds of ideals are always present in people's lives: our hopes and our current reality. How should UUs bridge the gap between our hopes and our realities? If we can engage that question, we can envision and shape the future of our religion with the consciousness of our past. It takes time and courage to answer such a question.

Hospitality does not necessarily change people, but it frees up the space in which people can embrace change. Transformational change can take place in our respective worlds. At this time, UUs have an opportunity to come to terms with who we are and where we stand. Persistent and gentle ongoing examination of self-identity and daily practices will help UU congregations to grow with authenticity as we find creative ways to continue to enrich our lives with offerings of worship, religious education, community, pastoral care, and outreach. It is not easy to reconcile our beliefs with how we live our everyday lives. Hospitality practiced daily, as a discipline, will open us up to the power and presence of the holy. Joseph Santos-Lyons, a seminarian and the UUA's Campus Ministry and Field Organizing director, writes,

> At church I feel connected to the wisdom and history of liberal religious people and membership in an intergenerational community that struggles with real life issues. My mind, heart, and soul are stretched to welcome new ideas, dreams, and passions for creating our beloved community.[7]

Isaiah 6:8 reminds us that each of us must take responsibility: "And I heard the voice of the Lord saying, 'Whom shall I send, and who will go for us.' Then I said, 'Here I am! Send me.'" May we be true to our liberal, idealistic, and visionary ideals. May we take the journey and stay the course.

Keeping Our Young People

It is a known fact that a large majority of UU children leave the movement when they grow up. Sometimes, the common belief goes, they return when they have children of their own; sometimes they do not. Often they continue to identify themselves as Unitarian Universalists but do not participate in the life of any congregation.[8] This broad trend continues despite considerable work in recent years in the young adult community on "bridging" youth as they grow out of youth programs. There are various opinions about the severity of the problem, but most UUs agree that it is a problem.

A common reason for young people to leave is that they find something lacking in the adult congregation. A conversation about this topic on a young adult discussion list indicates a longing for a more "spiritual" and "participatory" experience, with "magic," "ecstatic joy and hopefulness." UU young adult leader Sharon Hwang Colligan notes that the missing quality is difficult to describe but vitally important. In her booklet *Children of a Different Tribe*, she describes a conversation with UU youth leaders:

> "Can you tell me what, specifically, you think is needed?"
> "*Conferences*," their leader said. Her body language put a universe into that one word.

"But what kinds of things at conferences?" I persisted.

She didn't know how to answer me. I was a fellow UU; I was supposed to know what *conferences* meant. She tried more meaningful glances, more urgent body language, more vivid energy exchanges. I persisted in asking for words.

Someone else tried. "You know. *Community*." Someone said, "Workshops." And then, "And uh, you know, worship and stuff."

I tried, but that was as far as we ever got. Four words. Conferences, Community, Workshops, Worship.

These were intelligent, beautiful young people trying to communicate about the experiences that formed the emotional, spiritual, and social center of their lives, and they could not find more than four words to say what it was.

That conversation stayed with me, haunted me. Their urgency, and their inability to speak. "There is such a need," they told me. *That* part they were able to say. "There is really an urgent need. Such a need for it."[9]

It is hardly surprising that a sudden transition from the warm and close community of YRUU to Sunday morning services can be a shock, as the following passage eloquently sums up:

> Of course services don't seem appealing to recent high school graduates, who not only have rarely been to one, but have spent the last four years in a candle-lit room in the church basement having really life changing intense conversations designed to push the outer limits of their spiritual selves. After that, we are expected to sit still and listen to the minister give rather dull sermon on social justice, joys and concerns about baby births and ailing elderly congregation members we've never met, and out of tune choral singing?[10]

The issue of losing our children is serious and well worth looking at thoroughly. There are two tragedies in the fact that so many young UUs drift away: The first is that the denomination loses their unique depth of experience and understanding of the tradition. The second is that the young people may miss the opportunity to develop to their full potential as religious people.

Perhaps UUs' hesitation to define ourselves clearly contributes to the drifting away of young members, because they cannot find anything in the faith to hold onto. A participant in one of our hearings complained, "My child said, 'I went to that church my whole childhood—what do they believe?'" We have heard a number of young adults suggest that one thing young people may be looking for and not finding in church is the depth

There are two tragedies in the fact that so many young UUs drift away: The first is that the denomination loses their unique depth of experience and understanding of the tradition. The second is that the young people may miss the opportunity to develop to their full potential as religious people.

dimension discussed in several places in this report. Many young adults who grew up UU have complained that Unitarian Universalism lacks depth, passion, or focus.

Born-inners, it seems, have some different religious needs than come-inners. For many newcomers, the experience of finding Unitarian Universalism is intoxicating enough; for someone from an oppressive background, it is wonderful to find a place where questions are welcomed and where nobody is cast out for believing the wrong thing. But for someone who grows up in the faith, the permission to question all matters of belief is not an earthshaking revelation—it is simply the way things are. Born-in UUs are often interested in exploring Unitarian Universalism and spirituality more deeply, but sometimes they cannot find a place for such exploration in the adult congregation. There is anecdotal evidence that many young people who grew up UUs either leave the movement or go into seminary. One theory is that seminary seems like the place to find the greater spiritual depth they seek. Those for whom it isn't tend to drift away.

The way UUs raise our children seems to prepare them for something completely different from what Unitarian Universalism actually offers. This suggests that UUs should change one or the other (or both). Since being raised UU is generally described as tremendously affirming and even life-saving, we should be reluctant to make changes that would threaten that experience. But how can we give our children more accurate expectations about what their experiences are likely to be in the adult UU world? Even better, can adult UUs change their world to give it more of the vital traits of young people's experience? How can we make our movement a worthy inheritance?

There are some things that UUs do very well in raising our young people. The experience of closeness and community that young people feel in YRUU, for example, has repeatedly been described as life-changing. The lessons of tolerance, respect, and acceptance our children learn shape the attitudes they carry for the rest of their lives, in ways they and their elders may not even be aware of.

However, there are also problems. One thing we heard repeatedly in our focus groups with youth was that adult UUs lack clarity about what they and the church believe, making it difficult for young people to determine their own beliefs. Some youth told us, "The grown-ups don't know what to believe either, so they can't help kids figure it out" and "Because we don't have a strong theological background, people just zoom to atheism; there's a vacuum. Like, 'We don't talk about God so then there isn't one.'" Part of the problem is the result of the lack of definition discussed throughout this report: we do not know what we believe in common, so we cannot teach it to our children. Part of it, though, is intentional: We have a common desire not to indoctrinate our children, to leave them free to determine their own truth. This is a noble aspiration, but have we taken it too far? Perhaps children don't get anything to hold onto *now* and they ultimately find themselves adrift in a confusing and frightening world. As a participant in one of our youth focus groups said, "Adults are concerned about influencing what kids believe, but being influenced by other people is how we figure out what we believe; it's the only way it can happen."

UUs need to give children what they need. Sometimes this means giving them answers. We don't have to tell them that these answers are the only answers or that they represent absolute truth. But the concept of developmental appropriateness is important. Sometimes a child (or adult, for that matter) needs the certainty of belief in the face of life's uncertainties.

Developmental appropriateness is also relevant in forms of worship. Children respond best to more experiential forms of worship such as ritual and sensory experience. In fact, many adults hunger for these dimensions of worship as well.

One youth in our focus group called adults to account for not living up to their ideals. Despite their professed concern for the ongoing religious search, she suggested that many adults don't make it a high priority: "Maybe adults are too caught up with running the church . . . to take time for spiritual exploration. Maybe we need more paid professionals to handle those things, allowing adults more time to process spiritual issues."

We also heard a lot of concern about segregation. Several youth who participated in our focus groups expressed a desire for more interaction between youth and adults because the two groups are too isolated from each other. Once people are fourteen or fifteen years old, these youth told us, they need to be incorporated into the larger community: "If you want to 'mind the gap,' you need to meld it more; bring the generations together, get youth and adults interacting more. Current structures create too much separation of the generations." This is not to say the church should do away with youth programming, but we should offer more points of contact rather than sequestering youth away in another building, only to bring them up on stage at GA to cheer them and send away again. (We note in passing that some of this integration is already happening in DRUUMM.)

There is something about the way youth do things that could fulfill a need for congregations, providing the depth, passion, and intensity some feel are lacking.

There is something about the way youth do things that could fulfill a need for congregations, providing the depth, passion, and intensity some feel are lacking. Young people seem closer to the organic sources of worship than many who have lived longer; they do a wonderful job of making ritual real. And youth and young adults *live* community. Many UUs value community above almost all else and struggle to make it real. The young people, by and large, *do* community in ways that adults can barely begin to emulate. They have learned what adults have subconsciously taught and taken it and made it their own. Adults would do well to learn from them.

Ultimately, this issue relates back to the basic study question. If UUs individually knew what they believed and were not afraid to talk about it, then at least our children would have a starting point. On a larger level, if we had more that we agreed on, we would have something better to teach. We need to acknowledge and name our theology and seek ways to teach it. We need to agree about what we do have in common and not be afraid to raise our children on those values and traditions. Adult UUs need to set their own houses in order if we are to be able to give our children something worthwhile. Lynn Ungar writes, "A religious education . . . is not something that just happens in a classroom in the basement or the RE wing while the adults are doing 'real church.' Religious education is the process of educating people in what it means to be religious, and it happens in everything we do at church—everything."[11]

Principles and Sources

One of the prominent places where UU theology is made manifest is in the Principles and Purposes, which were adopted as the Unitarian Universalist bylaws by the 1984 and 1985 General Assemblies and further amended in 1995.

It is important to recall that the Principles and Purposes document was crafted and adopted as a unified piece with four distinct segments: an opening covenant, seven Principles, six Sources, and two concluding paragraphs that serve as a benediction to the overall text. The Principles are frequently recited in worship and often printed on orders of worship and in newsletters; they are adapted in the place of individual congregational covenants and prominently displayed in the front of the UU hymnal. They have also been reformulated as a series of "Unitarian Universalists believe" statements for children in religious education classes.

The results of our Commission on Appraisal worship survey clearly demonstrate that the Principles and Purposes have become a common expression of UU shared faith. One of the questions asked of each congregation was, "What written statement of purpose or description of your congregation regularly appears on your orders of service or other communications?" Even though the question explicitly refers to a statement specific to the congregation, 56 of the 370 responding congregations reported that the UUA's Principles (or in one case, those of the Canadian Unitarian Council) serve that function for them. Another 86 regularly use the Principles in addition to a statement specific to the congregation. Four more regularly print selections from or adaptations of the Principles in their congregational publications.

The exceptional popularity of the Principles as a guiding statement of common commitment among individual Unitarian Universalists has been surprising. The committee that steered the process leading to near-unanimous adoption of the Principles and Purposes never anticipated the various uses to which their work would be put. Their charge was simply to propose an amended statement of purpose for the Bylaws, replacing the statement adopted at the time of consolidation in 1961—a document that many denominational activists had come to view as dated in terms of language and political fashion. However, as Warren Ross comments in *The Premise and the Promise*, "To an astonishing extent today's Principles and Purposes . . . have won a lasting place in Unitarian Universalist hearts and have been woven intimately into the fabric of our denominational life."[12]

The Commission holds that the unifying energy of the Principles and Purposes was inspired, at least in part, by a widely felt desire for religious definition, for some concrete statement of common identity as Unitarian Universalists. In practice, then, the Principles and Purposes have emerged as one symbol of unity amid theological diversity, summarized in the "covenant to affirm and promote . . . respect for the interdependent web of all existence of which we are a part."

Over the years, both Unitarians and Universalists have claimed that humanity is "part and parcel of the universe," to employ Ralph Waldo Emerson's phrase. However, as our faith has been collectively practiced, we have majored in individualism and minored in community.

The process and language of the Principles and Purposes represented a huge, historic shift from emphasis on independent belief toward corporate covenant. The complete text of the final document includes but also transcends our predisposition toward radical autonomy, thus enabling us to forge a more cohesive religious presence—what our post–World War I Unitarian and Universalist forebears, John Haynes Holmes and Clarence Russell Skinner, each described as the quest for the "Beloved Community." The present document marks a full-blown recognition that interdependence is an observable reality in the biological and physical domains of the cosmos as well as a pursuable objective in the social and religious realms.

The Principles and Purposes do an exemplary (though neither perfect nor complete) job of stating UUs' essential unity of affirmations and wellsprings without suggesting uniformity of thought or conformity of behavior.

The Principles and Purposes do an exemplary (though neither perfect nor complete) job of stating UUs' essential unity of affirmations and wellsprings without suggesting uniformity of thought or conformity of behavior. In light of this watershed text, Unitarian Universalists can speak proudly about their high, holy, and common ground as a religion without mandating that any stand on precisely the same piece of turf, for clearly "a free and responsible search for truth and meaning" remains central to the UU way of doing religion.

The Principles and Purposes launch with a pivotal opening line: "We, the member congregations of the Unitarian Universalist Association, covenant to affirm and promote. . . ." The stage for "living the interdependent web" is set.

In a creedal faith, individuals are tied together by one set of beliefs; in a covenantal faith, they are bound by faithfulness to vows. As covenanters, we contend that we can better shape and stretch the Unitarian Universalist faith within the caring critique and embrace of community. Consequently, whenever sister and brother Unitarian Universalists and congregations have explored and embodied our common Principles and Purposes, however imperfectly, over the past two decades, actual and mystical linkages have been forged among us. UUs are united across our differences of class and capacity, color and conviction, whenever we commit to living the interdependent web.

Promises and Covenant

Mutual promises flow from a shared covenant and draw Unitarian Universalists closer to our unifying core than individual claims can manage. Unitarian Universalism summons us to "pledge our troth" (an old-fashioned phrase that marries both truthfulness and trust) to one another, forging our individual religious journeys together.

Promises must be risked openly and publicly, unlike beliefs, which can be held in the privacy of one's own soul. Promises are fulfilled only in communal life. Promises require companions and signal institutional allegiance.

Promises remind us that we are connected and beholden to sisters and brothers in our chosen faith. We are spiritual kin, bound together in the interdependent web. Promises support partnerships through fair and foul weather. Promises foster and sustain beloved communities.

In reality, congregations, like couples, can crack and rupture for plenty of legitimate reasons. However, breakups frequently occur because life appears greener elsewhere, because conflicts escalate without redress, or simply because of boring stretches. Hence, mature promise-making encourages partners and parishioners to calm down, breathe deeply, and stay at the welcome table.

Unitarian Universalist minister David Blanchard penned wisdom applicable to covenantal bonds of all sorts in his meditation manual *A Temporary State of Grace*:

> Do more than simply keep the promises made in your vows. Do something more: keep promising. As time passes, keep promising new things, deeper things, vaster things, yet unimagined things. Promises that will be needed to fill the expanses of time and of love . . . keep promising.[13]

Promises remind us to remain firm yet flexible, to choose again what we chose before. Promises prompt us to keep an evergreen awareness in our interpersonal and institutional lives, to grow where we are planted, and, as necessary, to do some repotting.

The following five promises spring from UUs' foremost covenantal commitment to living the interdependent web. This list is meant to be evocative, not exhaustive, to stir fellow Unitarian Universalists to make additional pledges that incarnate their theology within their congregations and in the larger world.

We Promise to Live Relationally

Note in the Principles and Purposes ever-widening circles from "the inherent worth and dignity of every person" to "human relations" to "congregations" to "society" to "world community" to "the interdependent web of all existence." In every circle of engagement, Unitarian Universalists are challenged to employ "the democratic process."

Located at the heart of UUs' promise to live relationally sits the third principle: "We affirm and promote acceptance of one another and encouragement to spiritual growth in our congregations." In Unitarian Universalism, *congregation* refers to a host of local designations, ranging from fellowship to church to society to community. Furthermore, UU institutional religion is embodied in the Church of the Larger Fellowship, whose members relate primarily via newsletters and correspondence.

As a faith, UUs have evolved, and wisely so, from the notion of tolerance to one of acceptance—a broader spiritual outlook. Authentic acceptance means living affirmations that liberate rather than enslave us and others. It signals an unfettered yet responsive religion, a distinction that lies at the core of effective promise-making.

Additionally, Unitarian Universalism is an encouraging instead of a despairing religion. When our days are dreary and crises bedevil us, spiritual kin step forward to lift us up or push us forward by offering affection and comfort.

UU spiritual growth takes place in multiple arenas, but primarily in our chosen communities of faith. Lamentably, Unitarian Universalists are prone to practice acceptance everywhere but in our own parishes, where we've been known to pick fights and nurse grudges with impunity. Parishes would do well to promise one another acceptance and encouragement. Acceptance affirms people as they are, and encouragement propels them toward who they might become—thus bringing UU theology to life.

Acceptance affirms people as they are, and encouragement propels them toward who they might become—thus bringing UU theology to life.

We Promise to Live Ethically

Protestant theologian Harvey Cox has often chided Unitarian Universalists for being thick on ethics and thin on theology. However, Cox may not realize that, although UUs are not theologically predictable, Unitarian Universalism at its truest is a religion bubbling in a stew of liberal theologies. As we put it, "The living tradition we share draws from many sources."

Nonetheless, UUs are indeed thick on ethics. The Principles and Purposes range from "justice, equity and compassion," to "a free and responsible search for truth and meaning," to "the right of conscience and the use of the democratic process," to "the goal of world community with peace, liberty and justice for all."

Unitarian Universalists aim to lead ethical lives of high character and conduct. Our journeys are steered from a moral compass. To enrich matters, UU ethical mandates are not separate from but integral to our religious reality. For UUs, protest and prayer are two sides of the same coin.

We Promise to Live Pluralistically

UUs follow a theologically interdependent path since we belong to a heritage that drinks from assorted fountains. Unitarian Universalists select the finest wisdoms "affirmed in all cultures." Religious pluralism is the denomination's peculiar slant. UUs aspire to live eclectically in the most resourceful sense, even though we fall short in practice.

UUs are religious hybrids—mystical humanists and naturalistic theists. We are grounded in Jewish and Christian lore, tempered by the traditions of skepticism and existentialism, and immersed in earth-based spirituality.

Newcomers to the UU religious heritage can borrow or blend from all six of the enumerated Sources (and any others of their own fashioning) in the Principles and Purposes text. Individual Unitarian Universalists are the final authors of their own religious identities and destinies, with companions in each beloved community doing likewise.

Traditional religions typically claim one primary source as definitive. In contrast, Unitarian Universalism does not rank its Sources according to revelatory importance. They are merely listed, with the assumption that each delivers distinct and necessary truths for thickening UUs' interdependence.

Along with Unitarian forefather Ralph Waldo Emerson, UUs insist "that the charm of life is this variety of genius, these contrasts and flavors by which Heaven has modulated the identity of truth."

We Promise to Live Evangelistically

Both the words *affirm* and *promote* in the Principles are essential to living the interdependent web. We *affirm*, as in state with fervor and clarity; and *promote*, as in publicize carefully. Affirm and promote are not passive terms; they entail action; they spell evangelism and social action. They oblige us to make our theologies real in the world.

Unitarian Universalists are notoriously nervous about being advocates, let alone ambassadors, for our free faith; it is tempting to minimize or bypass altogether the word *promote*. But in a world rife with political and religious fundamentalisms, it behooves religious liberals to engage in vigorous outreach, to spread our gospel to the ends of the earth. It is precarious and ineffective to affirm and promote merely as individuals. UUs need a unified, corporate witness affirming and promoting hopeful, inclusionary, and compassionate values.

But UU Principles and Purposes go further. The benedictory paragraph that follows the Sources furnishes marching orders: "Grateful for the religious pluralism which enriches and ennobles our faith, we are inspired to deepen our understanding and expand our vision."

In the mature religious journey, reaching within and reaching beyond are yoked movements. Evangelism is the outcome of embodied theology.

Evangelism is the outcome of embodied theology.

Note that the Purposes of the Unitarian Universalist Association do not stop with meeting the needs of existing congregations. UUs are instructed to "organize new congregations" and to "extend and strengthen Unitarian Universalist institutions and implement its principles." As adherents who pledge to live evangelistically, we aren't permitted to hide our flaming chalices under a bushel; rather, we're commissioned to light fires in cold rooms around the globe.

Evangelism signals Unitarian Universalism's unyielding promise, as a full-service religion, always to stretch our interdependent web to encircle yet one more sister or brother. Evangelism ensures, as President William Sinkford remarks, that "no one is left behind."

We Promise to Live Globally

The fifth and final promise beckons UUs to become co-sustainers with all living entities, stewards of the fragile spacecraft Earth. It is linked with the seventh Principle: "We affirm and promote respect for the interdependent web of all existence of which we are a part."

It is sobering to recall that this prominent Principle was vilified by many when it was first proposed—partly because it was a late addition proffered by a rump group of perceived interlopers, but also because it appeared too metaphysical in the eyes of theological centrists. Now this extraordinarily popular Principle serves as both apex and anchor for the "sacred seven."

The operative verb *respect* entails holding the interdependent web in holy regard or reverence. Respect also means refraining from interference.

Yet even more is required. We are called to respect the "web of all existence," not just those segments of the "great living system" that appeal to our chauvinistic concerns.

The Principle ends with the phrase "of which we are a part." Consequently, humans are not considered life's final accomplishment but an integral part of the whole. We need to acknowledge, not just intellectually but viscerally, that we are products of nature. We are of the soil, the sea, and the air. Created of the same stuff, we are interdependent. Literally, we all "hang together."

It is both proper and unifying that the Purposes and Principles document exacts a final promise: "As free congregations we enter into this covenant, promising to one another our mutual trust and support."

Unitarian Universalist congregations, as adept riders of paradoxes, are summoned to willingly fetter themselves. In short, we freely enter into covenant. And once entwined in covenant, what do we do? We discuss and dance, celebrate and serve, and keep on promising.

"Mutual trust and support" are perhaps the holiest human gifts, and utterly necessary as we boldly companion and empower one another in the sacred task of tending and mending the interdependent web of all existence.

Notes

1. Paul Rasor, in Marjorie Bowens-Wheatley and Nancy Palmer Jones, eds. *Soul Work: Anti-racist Theologies in Dialogue* (Boston: Skinner House, 2003), 109.
2. *Webster's New Universal Unabridged Dictionary*, 2nd ed. (New York: Simon & Schuster, 1983).
3. Sharon Blevins (media campaign test coordinator for All Souls Unitarian Church in Kansas City, MO). "The Uncommon Denomination," speech at GA 2003.
4. *Singing the Living Tradition*, reading 705.
5. Howard Thurman, *The Growing Edge* (Richmond, IN: Friends United Press, 1956), 146.
6. Joan D. Chittister, *Wisdom Distilled from the Daily: Living the Rule of St. Benedict Today.* (San Francisco: HarperCollins, 1991), 130-131
7. Michael Tino, *Finding a Spiritual Home: Unitarian Universalism for Young Adults* (Boston: UUA, 2003). Available online at www.uua.org/pamphlet/3603.html.
8. The figure usually cited is that 90 percent, or sometimes 85 percent, of children who grow up as UUs do not remain UUs as adults. This seems to be an anecdotal figure, which is widely accepted and quoted as the truth. The closest thing to concrete evidence to support this that we could find is a Commission on Appraisal survey done in 1989, which indicated that 14

percent of adult UUs grew up as UUs. This is a somewhat different assertion. The 90-percent figure seems to have become a bit of an urban legend.

9. Sharon Hwang Colligan, *Children of a Different Tribe*, 23. Available online at www.circlemaker.org/cdt.html.

10. Posting to a young adult discussion email list.

11. Lynn Ungar, "A Carefully Loaded Ship," *Journal of Liberal Religion* vol. 1, no. 1 (October 1999). Available online at www.meadville.edu/ungar_1_1.html.

12. Warren Ross, *The Premise and the Promise: The Story of the Unitarian Universalist Association* (Boston: Skinner House, 2001), 91.

13. David S. Blanchard, *A Temporary State of Grace* (Boston: Skinner House, 1997), 62.

Conclusions and Recommendations

The UUA is an intentionally noncreedal religious body, and individual freedom of belief and conscience are central to UU values; thus we cannot make universal statements of faith that apply to all of us individually. Yet it is possible to suggest statements that are central and uniting. Here are a few:

As Individuals
- We base our convictions upon our own experience of the depth dimensions of life, which is richer and more complex than any words or concepts we use to describe it. Individuals experience this depth encounter in relationship to many and different aspects of life and name it differently. For some, the most powerful encounters are with aspects of themselves, or mentors, or others within community; others find them in the natural world or in inspired writings or ideas. Some define what they encounter as "God" or "mystery"; some use other words. Such profound encounters often have the power to transform us as we cannot willfully transform ourselves.
- We embrace a sense of possibility—an openness to what is unknown—the not-yet, the new, the different—an openness that fosters qualities of authenticity, curiosity, creativity, courage, and compassion, all of which nurture hope and healing in our world.
- We are committed to being people of character. We value education, examples, and disciplines that strengthen our ability to be responsible

citizens of the earth and our society—honest and committed, kind and generous, reasonable and persistent, courageous when need be and able to be true to our values in the face of social pressure to be otherwise.

As Communities
- We claim a vision of religious community that protects and respects individual freedom, fosters acceptance (historically, "tolerance"), and supports an active quest for greater understanding and deeper meaning and purpose. We strive to create a place where the authority of the individual conscience is acknowledged and cultivated, where disciplined inquiry is encouraged a community friendly to wisdom from the sciences and social sciences as well as to the wisdom of many faith traditions.
- We share a conviction that wisdom emerges from the process of dialoguing across our differences in community. In dialogue we are challenged to examine our assumptions and to be open to growth and transformation, and to develop skills in communication that serve our world well.
- We are committed to religious community as a place where we work together for a more just and compassionate world. It is not enough to gather in a safe, supportive sanctuary for ourselves alone. We must be visible and present to those who need us. Our experience of religious community strengthens us to go forth into the world empowered to make a difference.

Toward the World
- We acknowledge a primary responsibility to value persons and to serve humankind—to affirm and promote "justice, equity, and compassion in human relations." Therefore we are moved to challenge societal assumptions and practices that are counter to those values.
- We affirm a vision of the natural world as an interdependent web, of which we are inextricably a part—not as dominators but as companions and at times protectors. Our cosmology draws heavily from the teachings of science. We acknowledge an ethical responsibility to foster sustainable use of the world's resources and to live in harmony with all beings.

In an important essay published in 2001, UU writer Kenneth A. Oliff cited commentary from nine individuals (Unitarian Universalists and others), as well as a part of the 1997 report of the Commission on Appraisal, from which he drew the following conclusion:

The most conspicuous element identified in these quotes is the absence of a principle of union in religious liberalism. This is variously expressed as a theological center, a common faith, a common story, or a shared system of beliefs. Most importantly, a principle of union is a shared understanding of what a church means theologically that moves beyond rejection and reactivity as a basis for religious liberalism.[1]

It was a similar concern about this conspicuous absence of a shared understanding of what Unitarian Universalism means theologically that motivated the Commission on Appraisal in October of that same year, after more than six months of deliberation, to choose the topic of the present study, originally formulated around the question: "Where is the unity in our theological diversity?"

The importance of this issue has been attested to by the extraordinary amount of interest expressed in our three-year exploration of it. We have been gratified and encouraged by this interest, by the engaged dialogues we have held with the many people who have attended our workshops and hearings across the country, by the letters and other communications we have received, and especially by the many sermons that have been preached and papers (and at least one book) published on the subject, which we have read with great appreciation. In addition, we value the input of all those who have contributed to formal and informal surveys circulated in conjunction with our study, and we are particularly grateful for the response to our worship practices survey, to which more than a third of UU congregations responded.

From the beginning we have said that if we accomplished nothing more than initiating a thoughtful, engaged, and widespread discussion of this important subject our effort would have been worthwhile. To that extent we have succeeded beyond even our own expectations, though perhaps an even stronger catalyst than our own efforts was UUA president Bill Sinkford calling us to a renewed "language of reverence" in 2002.

But mindful of a popular early twentieth-century witticism—defining a Unitarian as someone who, given the choice between going to Heaven or to a discussion group about Heaven, unhesitatingly chooses the latter—we would disappoint no one more than ourselves if we were to rest content with the mere conclusion that "more dialogue" is needed on this important subject. We do not discount the importance of an ongoing conversation, which is why this report includes some guidelines for group discussions based on what we have learned from our own; they are designed to be helpful in making such discussions more truly open and engaged, as well as perhaps a little deeper and more probing, than they might otherwise be.

However, the Commission hopes for more—of itself and for the Association—with this report. *Diversity*, both cultural and religious, has been the watchword of the movement's recent past, and insofar as that indicates UUs' sincere desire to be truly open and welcoming of people of all sorts into the UU fellowship, that emphasis is all to the good. And certainly the world today sorely needs communities of faith, indeed communities of all kinds, that are models of inclusion and pluralism where human differences do not divide. But diversity by itself, important as it is, is an insufficient institutional goal. More pressing is the question of what we are calling people into community *for*. If we are a community, what is the common unity that binds us together? And if we are a religious community, shouldn't we be able to articulate theologically and religiously what it is that unites us?

As we have wrestled with this question, we have differed among ourselves even regarding how best to ask it. We would emphasize, however, that our goal is not to invent or create the answer but rather to discover it; that is, to articulate as best we can, not what our underlying unity should be, but what it is. In short, we want to be primarily *de*scriptive, not *pre*scriptive.

If we are a religious community, shouldn't we be able to articulate theologically and religiously what it is that unites us?

If we have been disappointed by anything in the process of this study, it has been the suspicion, and in a few isolated cases even the hostility, with which some have greeted it and us. The fear has been expressed that we want to create or promote a common creed or its equivalent. Others have suspected us of ulterior motives, including the desire to exclude on theological grounds one or another of the expressions of religious thought current among UUs. Such fears are somewhat ironic. Our primary concern and motivation have been to discover and articulate what we hold in common, and there is hardly any principle or value more widely shared among UUs than that of individual freedom of belief. The Commission would agree with Ken Oliff that "the strength of the contemporary liberal church lies in its openness, its respect for difference, and in the value that the church places on the sanctity of individual conscience." But we also agree with his observation that "where the church falls short is in its lack of clarity regarding an explicit theological vision, and an ensuing ambiguity regarding mission, purpose and commitment."[2]

Such ambiguity and a concomitant tentativeness in articulating what UUs are about religiously may be our greatest liability and the greatest obstacle to achieving our potential as an empowering and liberating faith for the twenty-first century. The fear that any such articulation somehow threatens the integrity or right of conscience of any individual is institutionally disabling and must be overcome by mutual trust and a sense of common purpose—the belief that UUs are joined together in religious association for more than merely instrumental reasons. As the 1997 Commission report asked, "While discarding the doctrine of Lordship, have we also lost a principle of union? Are we in a community of congregations merely to simplify the delivery of services?"[3]

While a great many would say that the answer to that last question is no, the Association's own Bylaws can be used to support the notion that its legitimate purposes are purely functional. The Bylaws say that the UUA is "a voluntary association of autonomous, self-governing local churches and fellowships . . . which have freely chosen to pursue common goals together." This assertion of congregations' independence can be read as a defiance of even the possibility of unity except at the margins. Those most in favor of the autonomy of local congregations tend to interpret the legitimate role, the "common goals," of the Association in limited and primarily practical terms: providing assistance in such areas as curriculum development, ministerial credentialing, and so forth.

While the concern to uphold congregational autonomy is legitimate, the first four decades of the Association's history have reflected an increasing desire to create a more organically connected community of congregations, as indicated by the following trends:

- the tendency to use the name *Unitarian Universalism* to describe one common and definite thing
- many historic Unitarian and Universalist churches adding or altering their names to include "Unitarian Universalist" (or in some cases "Universalist Unitarian")
- the overwhelming majority of UU churches adopting and treating as "official" the same hymnal when it was produced by the UUA
- the adoption of the Principles and Purposes of the UUA Bylaws as the common expression of a common faith, recited in worship and/or prominently printed on orders of worship, adopted in the place of congregational covenants, and prominently placed at the head of the hymnal (where Christian churches commonly locate the Apostle's Creed), as well as its reformulation as a series of "Unitarian Universalists believe. . . ." statements for children in religious education classes.

In practice the Principles have emerged as a symbol of unity. The irony is that they were intended primarily as a statement of *broad inclusiveness*; that is, of a wide and even all-embracing diversity appropriate to the bylaws of a religiously heterodox movement but theologically neutral to the greatest extent possible, and religiously eclectic with regard to the sources of UU tradition. In the words of the Committee chair, Walter Royal Jones Jr., "We really wanted to assure everyone that no point of view was going to be left out. We wanted to say to everyone, 'You belong.'"[4] In carrying out that intent they notably succeeded. The Hymnbook Resources Commission, in the preface to the new UUA hymnal in 1993, acknowledged the importance of the Principles and Purposes "as the touchstones of our decision to proclaim our diversity."[5]

The penultimate sentence of the current Principles reads as follows: "Grateful for the religious pluralism which enriches and ennobles our faith, we are inspired to deepen our understanding and expand our vision." This statement, however, begs the question at the center of this report: What is the substance of "our faith"? Just what is enriched and ennobled by the religious pluralism for which we are grateful? If we say to anyone or everyone, "you belong," what is it that they are invited to belong to?

These are the questions with which we have grappled in preparing this report. Lengthy though it is, it represents only the first step in what we envision as an ongoing, denomination-wide focus and effort. Below are recommendations we have formulated, based on our observations and deliberations. Some are intended for the Association as a whole, some for congregations or other bodies within the Association, and some for individual UUs.

Focus on Theology as an Association

The Commission recommends that the Association as a whole mobilize a denomination-wide effort to develop and articulate what shared commitments the UU faith calls us to affirm as well as what challenges we face at this particular time.

The Commission recommends that the Association as a whole mobilize a denomination-wide effort, building upon the findings of this report, to develop and articulate a deeper understanding of who Unitarian Universalists are as a religious people and what shared commitments the UU faith calls us to affirm as well as what challenges we face at this particular time.

At least three models from the past offer examples of how such a large-scale project might be undertaken: the development by the Western Unitarian Conference in the nineteenth century of a statement of "Things Commonly Believed Among Us"; the creation of the original Commission of Appraisal, which led to the publication of *Unitarians Face a New Age* in 1937; and the process followed near the time of denominational consolidation by several panels, resulting in the publication of *The Free Church in a Changing World* over forty years ago. It has now been twenty years since the original adoption of the Purposes and Principles in the UUA Bylaws. This report represents an effort in what we believe is the right direction, undertaken with necessarily limited resources. But its reception, combined with the strong response to President Sinkford's call for a renewed language of reverence, may be taken as indicators of the interest in and desire for a new focus on our religious identity, mission, and promise.

In indicating the three models mentioned above, we do not recommend any of them as entirely suitable for the present instance, but features of each could be considered. It seems clear to us that in our present situation whatever process is adopted would have to combine both widespread individual and congregational participation to be successful. It would have to be an open process that would also take full advantage of the wisdom of respected theological thinkers and religious leaders, both within and outside the movement.

At a minimum we recommend that at least one General Assembly in the near future be devoted to a theme such as "Theology and the Unitarian

Universalist Mission," or alternatively, that an intentional focus on theology become a regular feature of GA programming. We urge the UUA Board of Trustees and administration to consider giving highest priority to this proposed process and endeavor.

Whether or not the Association takes up the proposal outlined above, there are several ways in which its purpose can be advanced. The Commission recommends that:

- individuals read this report thoughtfully and encourage others to do the same
- congregations use this report as a sourcebook for adult education programming and discussion groups
- districts organize meetings to discuss issues and concerns raised in this report
- UU organizations of religious professionals, at all levels, consider themselves pacesetters in doing the work of theological reflection and analysis within their respective memberships, and to motivate and encourage others in this endeavor. Specifically that the Association of Church Administrators, LREDA, UUMA, and the UU Musician's Network intentionally address the underlying question and findings of this report in their respective continental, district, and chapter gatherings
- other organizations and entities take note of the specific recommendations herein that call for their attention and response

Develop Worship Resources

The Commission recommends that the UUA create and administer a collection of resources for use in theologically welcoming worship. They should be modeled on the kinds of materials formerly available through the Worship Arts Clearinghouse, one of several attempts by the UUA or smaller entities within it to provide and disseminate materials that could support the creation of rich and meaningful UU worship. These attempts have been short-lived, often because they were undersupported, underfunded, and haphazardly administered. None of these collections was intentionally theologically diverse. Few laypersons and equally few ministers are adequately prepared to plan worship that is inviting and acceptable to UUs of all theological stripes without reducing worship to the least common denominator in a way that leaves everyone in attendance unoffended but also unfulfilled. A collection of materials showing best practices in worship that is not only theologically inclusive but also appealing across differences of generation, personality, learning style, and so on, would be of great benefit to UU congregational life. Only the UUA, preferably in cooperation with the Canadian Unitarian Council and the International Council of Unitarians and Universalists, has adequate resources to create and administer such a collection.

Encourage Theological Literacy

The Commission found a need for deepening and clarifying UU theological understanding, individually and collectively. We consider it vital that leaders in the movement educate themselves and their congregations to a higher level of theological literacy. How many UUs have a clear idea of how liberal Christianity, or humanism, or even contemporary science has evolved over recent decades? We encourage people to "build their own theology," but do we give them enough tools—both through the creation of new ones and the utilizations of existing ones—to help them to think about their life experience theologically? Such tools should include language, concepts, and some sense of the dynamic history of ideas.

The Commission recommends the development of an adult religious education UU history curriculum from the point of view of the development of ideas, the history of theology, and contemporary Unitarian Universalism as part of a continuous tradition. This could include sections specifically designed for use in new-member classes.

The Commission recommends that the Department of Ministry and Professional Leadership Staff prepare a questionnaire to develop a contemporary and educational theological profile for congregations in search to use in evaluating the fit with a potential new minister. Religious naturalism, pragmatism, and process theology and philosophy need to be included, although an overall goal would be to de-emphasize traditional labels in favor of lifting up underlying assumptions.

The Commission recommends the creation of one or more user-friendly, topical readers consisting of material written by Unitarian, Universalist, and UU thinkers, past and present. In the process of data collection, we noted that few laypersons, when asked about influential teachers in their lives, mentioned Unitarians or Universalists beyond their own families and ministers. Instead, they turned to Eastern-influenced popular writers and popular psychology. Beyond Emerson and Thoreau, UUs do not know our own exemplars and what they thought about theological questions. The Commission will entertain the possibility of undertaking compilation of the first such collection itself.

After developing resources reflecting UU heritage, it could be helpful to develop further resources, also topical, that give congregations and congregants easy access to the thinking of others who are kin to us in their points of view as well as some counterviews.

Promote Spiritual Practices

The Commission recommends that ongoing efforts to develop and educate congregational members about UU-compatible spiritual practices be continued and extended. Unitarian Universalists vary in their desire for spiritual depth, and in their tolerance for activities and events intended to promote spiritual depth. An organizational structure is needed through which those with a greater need for spiritual depth can achieve it without imposing their wishes on those with a lower level of need.

In most UU congregations, the Sunday morning worship service is the only opportunity for truly corporate worship. While some congregations have other services on a regular basis—such as Evensong and midweek Vespers—this is not typical. In some congregations, small groups explore spirituality together, but these are usually limited in their focus. For example, there may be a Buddhist sitting group or a women's spirituality circle that draws largely on neopagan sources and practices. While clearly compatible with our UU Sources, these sorts of gatherings need to be planned carefully and thoughtfully so as to avoid the specter of cultural misappropriation and be truly consistent with a free and responsible search for truth and meaning. Many UU congregations offer adult religious education opportunities, but a cursory review of the existing curricula shows that they are slanted toward the intellectual and the historical and include few opportunities for the achievement of spiritual depth. There is no clear path of devotional, meditative, or spiritual practice that is made available through most UU congregations.

We have been told many times, over the course of our formal study process and also through personal conversations, that many UUs see seminary as the only way to explore what it means to be a UU in a deep and committed way. Many people have told us that as soon as they started to take their Unitarian Universalism more seriously, other people around them began to ask when they were going to enter the ministry. Is it true that seminary is the only opportunity for a UU to explore deeply what this faith is and how to live it?

Let us consider a hypothetical example from another tradition for the sake of comparison. An Episcopalian woman who does not feel called to the priesthood feels a need to explore her faith to a deeper degree than what is achievable through the standard Sunday morning service. In most Episcopal parishes there are additional opportunities for worship during the week. There are small groups and classes whose purpose is spiritual, not intellectual, exploration. There is a clear and concrete devotional practice that she can draw on and incorporate into her daily life. There are retreat centers to which she can go for intensive experiences. She can attend retreats at monastic communities, become a lay member, or even join as a full, avowed member of the community.

The Commission recommends that ongoing efforts to develop and educate congregational members about UU-compatible spiritual practices be continued and extended.

UUs' theological ancestors had some parallel resources to draw upon. The Universalists had a tradition of publishing prayer books and other texts for private or family devotional use. The Unitarians published an annual *Lenten Manual*, a tradition that has continued in a more generic way up to the present. On at least two occasions in modern Unitarian and Universalist history, quasi-monastic groups have formed: the Universalist Humiliati in the 1950s and the UU Congregation of Abraxas in the 1970s and early 1980s, both of which were formed in part to provide opportunities and practices for the achievement of spiritual depth.

There are many signs of a renewed interest among UUs in opportunities and practices for the achievement of spiritual depth. In 1999, Skinner House published a collection of essays on everyday spiritual practices.[6] The 2004-2005 Skinner House catalog includes new titles on memoir writing and prayer as spiritual practices. At the 2004 General Assembly, promotional flyers were distributed for an organizing group called Chalistry, a group that began as an Internet discussion board called "UU Nuns."

At the same time, there are also preliminary signs of a backlash against these sorts of practices by UUs who are uncomfortable with them or have no personal interest in them. Many feel that such practices are being foisted upon them in the context of corporate worship or that they are being disparaged by other UUs because they feel no need for such practices.

Without a means of spiritual exploration through communities and practices, the church will continue to lose youth, young adults, and older adults who feel spiritually unfulfilled by standard UU fare. At the same time, UUs need to take great care in administering and promoting such communities so as not to drive away those folks who see their UU congregation as their bastion of protection against these very things in the larger society.

A theme of triumphalism runs through the history of American UUs—a sense that the latest UU trend is the next logical step in an evolutionary process of "onward and upward forever," and that the old trend is inherently flawed and outdated. The Unitarian Congregationalists triumphed over the Trinitarian Congregationalists. The liberal Unitarians triumphed over the conservative Unitarians. The transcendentalist Unitarians triumphed over the orthodox Unitarians. The ultra-Universalists triumphed over the restorationist Universalists. The "new world religion" Universalists triumphed over the Christian Universalists. The humanists triumphed over the theists. Now there is concern that UUs who feel a strong need for spirituality will triumph over the humanists. Hearkening back to one of the quotes with which this study opened, UU history can be seen as that of a succession of people losing their church.

There is a need for humility and understanding on all sides and by all factions. There is a need to take both the Universalist trio of faith, hope, and love and the Unitarian trio of freedom, reason, and tolerance seriously. When it comes to the latter, we need to be honest with ourselves about how tolerant we actually are and what it will take to be as truly tolerant as we so frequently claim.

While spiritual practices tend to be personal and private, the well-being of a community is also a function of the well-being of its members. By developing specifically UU resources on spiritual practices, the church will provide a source of fulfillment for current members—especially youth and young adults, who feel a need for spiritual experience and who may otherwise leave UU ranks to find it. This will also provide another attraction to and means of entry into the UU community for visitors and others from the larger society. There need to be opportunities for interested individuals to explore issues of spiritual depth without committing to a three-year seminary program.

Structures to support individuals in the use of such practices are also necessary. Congregations can create supportive environments based on a small-group ministry model. Clusters of congregations and districts can provide a context within which intercongregational efforts such as classes and retreats can be organized. These events would be especially beneficial to small congregations, which may lack the critical mass of people needed to maintain such efforts locally. The camps and conference centers and the theological schools could also provide retreats centered on spiritual practices. UUs already use the retreat format with great success for trainings, especially those related to religious education and youth services; the same kinds of schedules and procedures could be adapted to spiritual practice training and opportunities. The theological schools could develop short-term educational experiences intended for the personal growth and enrichment of laity rather than the training of ministers. Building upon the existing distance-education programs of Starr King School for the Ministry and Meadville-Lombard Theological School could provide a source of enrichment for the laity as well as a source of enrollment for the schools. Events like Summer Institutes, Winter Institutes, General Assembly, and other similar gatherings of UUs could have more extensive spiritual practice opportunities and tracks. For those who wish to explore their faith deeply and over an extended period of time, some form of monastic, quasi-monastic, or communal environment, perhaps drawing on older organizations like the Congregation of Abraxas for inspiration, could be a tremendous opportunity for individuals as well as a source of reinvigoration for the congregations to which those individuals return.

The Commission recommends that the UUA take steps to ensure that UU congregations are theologically safe places.

Protect Theological Diversity in Our Congregations

The Commission recommends that the UUA take steps at all levels to ensure that UU congregations are theologically safe places. In recent years, safety for specific kinds of people has been an area of attention for the Association and its congregations. We have put a great deal of effort into trying to make our congregations safe and welcoming for all sorts of people, especially in terms of race and sexual or gender identity. UUs have engaged in self-study to find the sources of prejudice, discrimination, and risk in our institutions, regulations, procedures, and attitudes. The Welcoming Congregations curriculum and resources provide good examples of what can be accomplished with intentionality and organization.

While such efforts are ongoing and incomplete, their effects to date have been positive. We on the Commission feel that a similar program needs to be undertaken to encourage our congregations to be truly welcoming and safe theologically. The UUA and its districts need to support congregations in exploring their implicit or explicit theological prejudices and develop plans to ensure that they are truly welcoming to and safe for UUs of all theological stripes, both those among the current membership and those who may be drawn to UU communities if they find them hospitable. Helping congregations become more theologically welcoming is one of the stated goals of the curricula currently under development by the UUA's Lifespan Faith Development Office; we see this as a good first step toward what we are recommending. A side benefit of these efforts will be better preparation for UU congregations to get along with other religious groups in their communities and cooperate with them in interfaith work on social justice and other issues.

With so much emphasis in recent years on spirituality, both within Unitarian Universalism and in the wider culture, it is perhaps not surprising that at least some of the many UUs who identify themselves theologically as humanists feel particularly embattled or marginalized. Because a few have raised concerns and questions about our motives and intentions as a Commission, we want to acknowledge their concerns and also explicitly affirm the significant contributions of the humanist tradition to Unitarian Universalism. The ability of humanists to knit together the disparate elements of their lives without a need to rely upon something supernatural is testimony to the power of human reason. It has also given UUs access to a vision of human rights that motivates us to work for justice.

It would be a serious denial of our intellectual heritage to allow the Humanist perspective to be marginalized as a source of our vision and strength. At the same time, we encourage humanists to consider that not all references to what might appear to be traditional religious language or belief signify the relinquishing of reason as a powerful element in UUs' lives, including our spiritual lives. Just as there are many languages in the world in which people may describe the realities of their existence, so there are many ways in which people give voice to their inner experiences. So long as they are not coercive or exclusive, they need not be barriers to UUs' worship and work together. Humanism has long held an honored place within the varieties of Unitarian Universalist religious expression, and we have no expectation that it will ever be otherwise.

Make Peace with Our Religious Past

The Commission recommends a direct approach to dealing with the theological reactivity that is so prevalent regarding Unitarian Universalism's Christian origins.

The roots of both Unitarianism and Universalism are historically Christian. That the majority of Unitarian Universalists today do not personally identify themselves as Christian does not change the fact of our origins. Furthermore, we have remained culturally Protestant, especially in our forms of worship, even as the focus of our worship (and even our use of the word *worship*) has changed. Despite this, negative reactions toward Christianity or anything identified as Christian are common in many if not most UU congregations. Many will read almost any scripture but the Bible. Although we may pay lip service to valuing our Christian heritage, we shy away from it in practice.

Denying our roots is not helpful to our perception of ourselves in either theory or practice. Such denial tends to make us react (even overreact) rather than respond to challenges. This can be a serious hindrance to the coalition building that needs to take place within the constellation of liberal religious traditions in an era of growing conservatism. It cuts UUs off from partaking fully of the wisdom to be found in the teachings of Jesus. And it makes us less welcoming to those whose minds are open, whose search is not done, but whose values have been shaped by that preacher's message—whether such people are inside our ranks already or not.

More generally, since feeling embattled or marginalized is not unique to UU humanists any more than to UU Christians or those of other deeply held beliefs, we need to address directly the fact that many come to our doors bearing the wounds of past encounters with organized religion. When those wounds go unrecognized, we foster the conditions for continued theological reactivity within our congregations. Development of more curricula like "Owning Your Religious Past" may be needed. It may also be useful to form small group ministry groups within churches specifically to address this issue.

A more recent phenomenon, which the Commission has come to label exoticism, is in effect the obverse of the reactivity mentioned above. Most commonly, while reactivity leads to dismissive attitudes toward Christianity, exoticism leads to an uncritical acceptance of other, less familiar traditions such as Buddhism or Hinduism. Both attitudes work against the thoughtfulness required for the accomplishment of true pluralism.

The Commission recommends a direct approach to dealing with the theological reactivity that is so prevalent regarding Unitarian Universalism's Christian origins.

Affirm Theological Diversity Among Ministers

The Commission also recommends that Ministerial Fellowship requirements for seminarians be examined with an eye toward allowing future ministers to go deeply into the theological traditions that most directly speak to them. In this vein, we need to recognize that different seminarians will bring different theological affinities and that we need to embrace and include such possibilities institutionally. Current MFC course requirements require all seminarians to take two courses in Judeo-Christianity, recommend two additional courses in Judeo-Christianity, and require one other course in "any additional religion." Such a structure clearly heavily emphasizes the UU Jewish and Christian heritage but discourages candidates who may wish to delve deeply into Buddhism, for example, or any other non–Judeo-Christian tradition. We propose that the MFC recommendation to "take two additional courses in Judeo-Christianity" be replaced by a suggestion that the student "take two additional courses in the religious tradition that most directly appeals to him or her, as a way of ensuring depth of exposure to and personal experience with that religion."

Foster Theology in Religious Education

The Commission recommends a systematic reexamination of existing religious education curricula for both children and adults, with an eye toward whether or not they teach Unitarian Universalist history theologically. How are we articulating the theology embedded in the narratives that are uniquely our own? Is the link to the theological roots of contemporary UU faith made explicit? If not, how can we strengthen and further emphasize that link?

The Commission recommends that curricula for young children include Bible stories as well as appropriate stories from other religious traditions. We owe it to our children to provide them with an appropriate background from which to communicate with schoolmates and friends. The Bible, however, is no longer part of the common educational culture, especially in the public schools. If anything, this aspect of religious education is more important than it was a generation or two ago, when we did use curricula that provided this background, including books like *From Long Ago and Many Lands* and *Old Tales for a New Day*.

The Commission recommends that the Lifespan Faith Development Department commission a child-friendly, attractive dictionary of theological and religious terms for use in families and church school, with CDs for computer use. (We note incidentally the need for greater use of alternative media and contemporary technology for communication and outreach at all levels of the Association.)

The Commission recommends the development of Faith in Action programs for junior and senior high school students, both within the UU community and beyond it. These should be carefully developed and implemented, perhaps collaboratively with the Unitarian Universalist Service Committee, and building upon the experiences of the Denver-area churches, which experimented with such a program in the 1980s. Numerous other denominations and individual congregations operate such programs; they can provide models.

Serve the Needs of Youth and Young Adults

The Commission recommends that the UUA commission a thorough study of why the church loses so many of its young people. Despite the difficulties involved, this should ideally include a survey of those who have left. A significant majority of children who grow up in Unitarian Universalist congregations do not remain in the church as adults. These people are a wonderful resource, and it would be of incalculable value to the denomination if we could retain more of them. While we recognize the good work being done by the Young Adult office and various Campus Ministry programs, which have apparently blossomed recently, this remains an important area of study and concern.

The Commission recommends that the UUA commission a thorough study of why the church loses so many of its young people.

Among the needs of young adults we have identified, several would be met by other recommendations in this report, for example the development of an adult religious curriculum on UU history, specifically focused on the development of theological and religious ideas, and more opportunities for spiritual development within congregations. Additional specific needs include supporting youth as they create and lead worship and address issues related to their moral and spiritual development.

Affirm Cultural Competency

The Commission recommends a continuing commitment at all levels of the Association to a deeper understanding and acceptance of cross-cultural issues between and among diverse peoples, especially those within our congregations and those who might join. Unitarian Universalism is changing; it is becoming more and more diverse—theologically, spiritually, and culturally. This is happening slowly, but steadily enough for us to consider the implications of this change.

Can we do a better job of welcoming others into our midst? Absolutely. In making a concerted effort to respect others, UUs have come to appreciate the roles of cultural sensitivity and cultural competency. Cultural competency values diversity and is willing to create a cultural self-assessment, to be aware of the differences at work among diverse cultures, and to institutionalize cultural knowledge. Cultural competency moves us toward being comfortable with and appreciating "the other" and creating policies and practices that ensure universal access to UU religious life in community.

Valuing diversity means respecting, not merely accepting, difference. When we sing a song out of cultural context, for example, we are not practicing cultural competency. More simply, if someone exploring the possibility of a new spiritual home calls a UU church to find out what time a service is and asks, "What time is Mass?" and the person answering the phone responds huffily, "We don't have Mass, we have a service, we aren't a Catholic church!" that person has not only been ungracious but simply unwelcoming.

Cultural competency includes the practices of humility, listening, patience, graciousness, and the holiest of curiosities. Rather than asking a newcomer, "What brings you here? How did you find us?" what if we were to ask as the Tibetans used to do, "And to what sublime tradition do you belong?"[7] However we do it, when we communicate graciousness, generosity, and openness, we represent Unitarian Universalism at its best.

Engage Theology

The Commission recommends that individual UUs and congregations acknowledge and deal with theological diversity rather than avoid it.

The Commission recommends that individual UUs and congregations acknowledge and deal with theological diversity rather than avoid it. Many adult UUs have told us that discussing theology and beliefs is not a frequent part of their congregational life. When pressed, most acknowledge that this is in part an attempt to avoid conflict and disagreement. A number of youth agreed with this assessment, adding that they felt many adults do not like to talk about what they believe because they are not sure what that actually is and are afraid of looking uninformed or unintelligent.

Sweeping UU theological diversity under the rug by refusing to talk about it in community is not a healthy way to approach the issue. Tolerance requires conversation, not avoidance. Talking about beliefs, learning from one another, and stimulating everyone's thinking through open and honest sharing of views should be encouraged in UU congregational life. During our focus group meetings with representatives from the UUA's affiliated theological identity groups, they all told us that life in a theologically homogenized congregation would be boring and would not provide sufficient stimulation to further personal growth. However, without open dialogue, the diversity that exists within the community cannot have this growth-stimulating effect.

Such open sharing needs to happen intentionally, with planning and forethought, through adult RE programs, small-group ministry, and other programmatic congregational events. This sort of planning will encourage further informal conversation. Many of the youth and young adults with whom we spoke told us that this dialogue, a common part of the shared experience of youth groups and YRUU events, is one of the main things they miss when they bridge to the adult community. Their mutual dialogue helps them to understand, learn from, and respect each other. This may be a place where the grown-ups can learn a great deal from the youth.

What Next?

With a topic such as this, it is not surprising that there has been considerable difference of opinion within the Commission, even about how to frame the question. One thing on which we have full agreement, however, is that this topic is vitally important for the health and future of our denomination. As mentioned in the first chapter, we have sometimes felt like we were breaking a taboo by raising this question. However, the tremendous response and enthusiasm with which many have greeted our efforts suggest that this is a taboo people are glad to see broken. It is like the story of the elephant in the living room: Everyone knows it is very large and very present, but there is an unspoken agreement to pretend it isn't there. The elephant for Unitarian Universalism is our lack of articulation about who we are and what we have in common, and the Commission believes the time is ripe to cease pretending it doesn't exist and actively confront it.

What might our faith look like twenty years from now if we move in the direction of the Commission's recommendations? We asked participants in focus groups to describe to us their dream of that future day. In the UU Buddhist group, one participant told us, "My dream is to be in a community where people have a depth experience of truth, then begin to see it in other places. They start to see there isn't only 'one way.' They have the flexibility to worship in different languages." Another imagines congregations where "diverse spiritual disciplines are explored in depth—everyone into it, but different practices for different folks. It would not be like going to the zoo or supermarket—a bit of this and that."

Near the beginning of this report, we quoted a participant in the Covenant of UU Pagans focus group when she said, "We [UUs] offer the hope of a spiritual journey, and we offer no tools to do it with." A future dream would be to develop and share those tools for enhancing our direct experience of embodied spirituality. Participants from the Process Theology Network sketched a vision of a church embracing the diversity of society: "Music needs to change to make people feel welcome and to reflect the diversity of the people. The people in the pews need to loosen up in general and embody what we're all about." Worship, according to this participant, needs to include elements that feed all the senses.

Someone in the UU Christian Fellowship group also hoped for a day when "People in the pews would look like those outside. We would share more common beliefs—holding ourselves accountable to something—so we could relax with our diversity." Another imagined that "It would be fun—the spirit would be alive. Worship would be more integrative and joyous, including drama, dance, music—drums and guitars—touch and all five senses. If the whole self is not in worship, it is not worth doing." A third pictured a place where "Membership meant you were a disciple of love and freedom."

From the UUs for Jewish Awareness focus group comes the dream of a community "well beyond tolerant and into open, welcoming and intrigued by diversity—a place to experience 'more ready wonder.'" A participant in the Humanist focus group offered this vision: "If we can get beyond our fears about expressing our diversity without either giving or taking offense, that's the work of peace and justice in the world."

What is remarkable about these visions of the future is that very few participants named elements that those in other groups would find unappealing. All these voices join together to create a vision of an open community, reflecting the diversity of society, where people can find tools to touch the depths of human possibility in a number of different ways. All value making people welcome and treating them with respect, encouraging imagination and flexibility, being spiritually multilingual and vitally alive. All express commitment to the work of peace and justice in the world, and to responsible cherishing of our natural environment. Most yearn for more nourishing theological articulations of our common ground, and would embrace the call for an embodied spirituality and the experience of "more ready wonder."

The Commission on Appraisal does not see this report as the end of a process; rather, we hope it will be a beginning. We have raised the issue, and asked many questions; now it is time for us all to engage collectively, thoughtfully, and respectfully, in the challenging process of searching for answers. What could our UU faith be like if our congregations truly became the safe and welcoming place we aspire to create? If we truly did honor and celebrate both our theological diversity and our sources of unity? If we were willing to commit to spiritual discipline as deeply as to spiritual freedom? "Whether we now have the seeds of a liberating faith is not really a question. Deluding ourselves into thinking that admiring the seeds will make them grow is the issue at hand," writes a contemporary UU prophet.[8] What marvels might be possible if we took these seeds and planted and tended them? What wondrous blossoms might arise?

All these voices join together to create a vision of an open community, reflecting the diversity of society, where people can find tools to touch the depths of human possibility in a number of different ways.

Notes

1. Kenneth A. Oliff, "Constructing a Commanding Vision of God for the Liberal Church," *The Unitarian Universalist Christian*, vol. 56 (2001): 13.
2. Oliff, 5.
3. Commission on Appraisal, *Interdependence: Renewing Congregational Polity* (Boston: Unitarian Universalist Association, 1997), 9.
4. Warren Ross, *The Premise and the Promise: The Story of the Unitarian Universalist Association* (Boston: Skinner House, 2001), 91.
5. UUA, *Singing the Living Tradition* (Boston: Beacon, 1993), vii.
6. Suggested by the work of Henry Nelson Wieman (1884-1975).
7. From Huston Smith, *Requiem for a Faith* (video) (Wellspring Media, 1997.)
8. Gordon McKeeman, personal communication, December 30, 2003.

2004 Statement of Agreements and Tensions

In the first chapter of this report, we presented the statement of agreements and tensions created by the AUA Commission of Appraisal in 1936 and asked a provocative question: "What would such a statement look like if an earnest effort to state plainly the areas of Unitarian Universalist points of agreement and disagreement were undertaken today?"

As an exercise, the Commission took time during the 2004 General Assembly to engage in just such a process. Each one of us individually created such a list, seriously attempting to think beyond our own narrow interests to our experiences with all of our Unitarian Universalist sisters and brothers. We took these individual lists and collated them, looking for themes and commonalities. Based on these themes, we created the list below.

We are including this document in our report with some trepidation, lest it receive an undue amount of attention and seriousness. This is the result of an exercise conducted by nine people; unquestionably, a different group of nine would create a very different list. The rationale behind including our list is to inspire the creation of other lists—at a congregational level certainly, and perhaps even at an associational level. A group of interested individuals within a congregation—or in a small congregation, the entire membership—could follow a procedure similar to this one. Such a document could be of great benefit in visioning and goal-planning, acculturating new members, guiding publicity efforts, and inspiring adult religious education offerings.

All the delegates at a General Assembly cannot reasonably replicate the process we followed. However, we believe a comparable statement created at an associational level, while much more difficult to craft, would be of great benefit to the UUA and its member congregations. The content of such a document undoubtedly would correspond more closely to the classical aspects of systematic theology than the current Principles do.

In summary: Please take this statement in the spirit it was intended. Go and do likewise.

Human Nature

We agree that all human beings have worth and dignity and must be respected.

We are optimistic about the human capacity for goodness but recognize that every person is capable of evil.

Knowledge and Revelation

We agree that revelation and knowledge come from many sources and that truth is always incomplete and evolving.

Reason

We agree that reason is a necessary part of religious inquiry and that the abilities of the human mind to think and choose must be brought to bear on religious questions in a disciplined and rigorous way.

We disagree as to whether reason is a sufficient route to understanding by itself or whether other processes that go beyond the boundaries of reason are necessary.

Freedom of the Individual

We agree that no one owns the truth, and that each person must be free to search for the truth in a responsible and disciplined way and to choose what to believe based on individual experience and conscience.

We disagree as to whether freedom itself is a sufficient basis for religious faith or for holding together a religious community.

Human Responsibility

We agree that human beings are responsible for creating a just, sustainable, and peaceful world through human capacities for forgiveness, nonviolent conflict management, cooperation, and community building.

We disagree as to what is necessary to create such a world, and the extent to which we are responsible for maintaining the status quo.

Value of Community

We agree that being a part of an inclusive and covenantal religious community is important to the formation of a healthy religious self.

We disagree as to whether the building of a beloved community or supporting the quest of the solitary individual is the true goal of our congregations.

Democratic Process

We agree that decision-making in our communities should follow a democratic model.

We disagree as to how to settle conflicts and how to preserve the rights of both the majority and the minority on any issue.

Nature of the Divine

We agree that the universe is an interdependent web, held together by a force (or forces) that can be understood in a variety of ways.

We disagree concerning how that force (or forces) should be named, and whether or not it possesses consciousness.

Interdependent Web

We agree that the natural world is a continuously evolving web of interdependence and mutuality and that human beings must respect the impact of our actions on the whole.

Source of Evil

We agree that evil is most commonly the result of human choices and actions. We disagree as to whether evil is solely of human creation.

Spirituality

We agree that awe, wonder, and love are necessary and healthy.

We disagree concerning the value of spirituality and spiritual practices for enhancing or engendering a sense of awe, wonder, and love.

Worship

We agree that it is important for a religious community to come together regularly for celebration, commemoration, mutual encouragement, and support.

We disagree as to whether that coming together should be called worship, and the extent to which it should involve ritual, song, texts, and other aspects of worship common to the world's traditional religions.

Institutions

We agree that religious institutions have value.

We disagree concerning the level of responsibility the individual has for the institution and whether institutionalization is important at more than a local level.

Sources of Authority

We agree that the conscience of the individual is the ultimate locus of religious authority.

We disagree concerning the degree to which the individual conscience should be informed, inspired, or critiqued by tradition and community.

Worship Survey

Some general results and interpretations of the congregational worship survey are discussed in the chapter on worship. The tables on the following pages give more detailed findings.

Table 1: Frequency of Special Theme Services

Reported Services	Number of Congregations That Offer	Percentage of Total Responses
Flower Communion/Ceremony	323	87.6
Christmas Eve	304	82.4
Children's/Religious Education	261	70.8
Water Communion/Ceremony	260	70.4
Passover Seder	130	35.1
Holy Communion	64	17.4
Bread Sunday	51	13.8
All Saints/All Souls/Day of the Dead	44	11.9
Thanksgiving (any form)	33	8.9
Solstice/Equinox	29	7.9
Easter	24	6.5
Youth	24	6.5
New Member (one or more)	20	5.4
Animal Blessing	18	4.9
High Holy Days/Yom Kippur	17	4.6
New Year/Fire Ceremony	15	4.1
Music/Choir (one or more)	14	3.8
Coming of Age	10	2.7
Earth Day	10	2.7
Martin Luther King	10	2.7
Ingathering/Homecoming	9	2.4
Memorial Day	9	2.4
Child Dedication	8	2.2
Christmas Pageant	6	1.6
Congregational Anniversary	5	1.4
Kwanzaa	5	1.4

Reported Services	Number of Congregations That Offer	Percentage of Total Responses
Pride	5	1.4
Advent/Advent Vespers	4	1.1
Canvass/Pledge	4	1.1
Guest at Your Table	4	1.1
Mothers' Day	4	1.1
Fathers' day	3	0.8
Jazz	3	0.8
Journey Toward Wholeness	3	0.8
May Day	3	0.8
Tennebrae	3	0.8
UU Service Committee	3	0.8
Volunteer Recognition/Appreciation	3	0.8
Bridging	2	0.5
Bring-A-Friend	2	0.5
Mardi Gras	2	0.5
Partner Church	2	0.5
Soulful Sundown	1	0.3

Table 2: Changes in Special Theme Services

Service Changes in Last 10 Years	Added	Eliminated
Water Communion/Ceremony	80	4
Flower Communion/Ceremony	56	2
Christmas/Christmas Eve	30	4
Passover Seder	29	14
Bread Sunday	21	2
All Saints/Day of the Dead	20	0
Communion	18	7
Children's Religious Education	17	5
Solstice/Equinox	16	0
All (unspecified by respondent)	13	0
New Year	10	0
Thanksgiving	10	0
Youth	10	0
High Holy Days/Yom Kippur	7	0
Memorial Day	6	0
Coming of Age	5	0
New Member	4	0
Easter	3	0
Journey Toward Wholeness	3	0
Kwanzaa	3	0
Martin Luther King, Jr.	3	0
Music/Choir	3	0
Advent Vespers	2	0
Congregational Anniversary	2	0
Coming Out/Pride	2	0
Earth Day	2	0
Maundy Thursday	2	1
All but Christmas Eve	1	0
Soulful Sundown	1	2
Partner Church	0	1
United Nations	0	1

The Commission received responses from 28 newly formed congregations, for which all services offered were new.

Table 3: Covenants Used in Worship

	Number of Congregations That Use	Percentage of Total Responses
Custom covenant or affirmation	46	27.7
Singing the Living Tradition 471 (Williams)*	42	25.3
Singing the Living Tradition 473 (Blake) **	41	24.7
Specific text not provided	13	7.8
Amalgam of *Singing the Living Tradition* 471 and 473	9	5.4
Singing the Living Tradition 472 (Ames) all adapted	4	2.4
Congregational mission or purpose statement	3	1.8
UUA Principles (complete or selected)	2	1.2
Singing the Living Tradition 448 (Robinson)	2	1.2
Singing the Living Tradition 434 (Anonymous)	1	0.6
Singing the Living Tradition 474 (Sen/Holmes) adapted	1	0.6
Winchester Profession	1	0.6
Unspecified from hymnal	1	0.6

* 15 use as published in *Singing the Living Tradition* and 27 use an adapted version.
**22 use as published in *Singing the Living Tradition* and 19 use an adapted version.

Tools for Theological Conversation

The following text is revised from a handout distributed to attendees of the Commission on Appraisal's workshop at the 2004 UUA General Assembly in Long Beach, California. The questions included are revised from those used with the focus groups discussed in the Methodology section of the opening chapter. We have formatted the questions, along with some basic information about the Commission and its work, in such a way that these pages could be photocopied and used as discussion materials for groups of Unitarian Universalists in our congregations, districts, seminaries, and other organizations and bodies. We recommend that groups using these questions have access to writing tools and paper or index cards for individual participants as well as newsprint or some other medium for taking notes that will be visible to the entire group. These questions are not meant to lead to definitive answers but rather to encourage UUs to "engage theology" in a mutually supportive and low-tension social situation. As such, several of the questions are intentionally light-hearted and seek to draw out a range of creative responses and interpretations.

Historical Background

In 1933, in the depths of the Depression, the Unitarian part of our movement was in such doldrums that its continued existence as an association seemed in question. In an attempt to find out what could be done to revitalize it, a group of concerned ministers and laypersons won endorsement from the 1934 Annual Meeting of the American Unitarian Association to form the Commission of Appraisal. The Commission, headed by Frederick May Eliot, examined every aspect of the Unitarian movement, from its churches and Boston headquarters to the values and needs of its individual members. As a result of its study, Unitarians Face a New Age, a dynamic new administration was created and there many in our movement experienced a feeling of rebirth. When the Universalist Church of America and the American Unitarian Association consolidated in 1961 to form the Unitarian Universalist Association, a Commission on (rather than "of") Appraisal was written into the bylaws of the new Association as a permanent body of the General Assembly. The Commission on Appraisal was given ongoing responsibility for evaluating the life of our movement and for making a report to the General Assembly on some aspect of our denominational life at least once every four years. It is the only non-Board and non-administration body given the freedom to look at and evaluate the life of our movement and the effectiveness of its structures.

Prior Reports include: *Belonging: The Meaning of Membership* (2001); *Interdependence: Renewing Congregational Polity* (1997); *Our Professional Ministry: Structure, Support and Renewal* (1992); *The Quality of Religious Life in Unitarian Universalist Congregations* (1989); *Empowerment: One Denomination's Quest for Racial Justice 1967-1982* (1983). (See www.uua.org/coa/reports.)

A Working Definition of Theology

While the root words of the term *theology* refer to "reason or discourse about God," these questions assume a much broader understanding of its meaning. In modern usage, the definition of theology is understood to include the full range of religious and philosophical beliefs (not just theistic ones) and humans' understanding of the meaning and purpose of life and of Ultimate Reality.

For discussions in a congregation, start with this question:

- What do you think holds this congregation together? What do the members share or have in common that makes it a community? [Respond individually in writing before discussing as a group]

For discussions in a group other than a congregation, start with this question:

- Think about what you identify as your Unitarian Universalist religious community--it may be your home congregation or it may be some other group with which you identify. What is this community? What do you think holds this community together? What do the members share or have in common that makes it a community? [Respond individually in writing before discussing as a group.]

Continue with these questions:

- Is there a religious practice or ritual that you believe many members of this community or congregation value? [Respond individually in writing before discussing as a group.]

- Imagine that you are filling out a form that asks this question [have in writing large enough for all in the group to read]: "What five words would you use to describe your personal religious beliefs?" [Respond individually in writing before discussing as a group.]

- Think once again about the religious community you identified earlier and the diversity of religious beliefs held by members of this community. Imagine what it would be like if, through some sort of magical event, those people suddenly became much more similar in their religious beliefs. Let's start with the hard question first: How would that religious community be better if people become more similar in their beliefs? How would it be improved? What current problems would go away?

- Now think about the reverse side of this magical event: How would the community be worse off than it was with all its diversity intact? What good things would be lost? What new problems would arise?

- Pretend that you are placed in suspended animation for twenty years as part of a science experiment. When you wake up and learn about how the world has changed, you discover that Unitarian Universalism is now the perfect religious organization or movement, and that community you identified has become the perfect religious home from your point of view. How would it have changed? What would it be like in terms of theology or religious beliefs?

The Parker Question

Near the end of the introduction to this report, we introduced a question raised by Starr King School for the Ministry president Rebecca Parker: *What features of Unitarian Universalism, if they were taken away, would leave something that is no longer recognizably Unitarian Universalism?*

During our workshop at the 2004 General Assembly, we asked attendees to think about this question individually and then discuss it with a partner before sharing with the larger group. We found the experience to be provocative and energizing for our participants.

We recommend a similar exercise for congregations and other groups of UUs. The similarities and differences that emerge from such a conversation may be very helpful to a congregation in the process of clarifying its self-definition for the purpose of developing a mission or vision statement, starting a ministerial search, or working through congregational conflict. Ministerial students should find it to be an engaging and educational experience. While groups of youth at camps and conferences may benefit from a discussion of this question, an intergenerational context may create especially enlightening discoveries.

Guidelines for Conflict Transformation

People often avoid discussions about theology because they anticipate conflict and feel they do not know how to create or engage in respectful dialogue. To lessen this anxiety, we offer some basic principles for such dialogue. Some elements are likely to be familiar already, such as those listed below under "Community Practices." Many congregations may already employ covenanting as part of their small-group ministry work. Such covenants assure the participants in a discussion that they will be respectfully heard.

The goal is to create a community of authentic listeners—respectful, attentive people who create the space for others to relate fully within the rich environment of religious engagement. The premise is that conflict and communication are neutral entities; what matters is how we deal with conflict and how we communicate. Attention is paid to identity, culture, and dialogue. The methodology seeks to give voice to the difficult questions we are called to answer. We want to lift up the hope of a strong, respectful community given to honest exchange that moves us forward with the profound understanding of "self as other, other as self." Its focus is on honoring the respect and dignity of all.

Community Practices: The methodology invites individuals to comfortably bring their whole selves to the meeting or gathering and build community before any business is conducted. We start each exchange with community practices that help create a safe space for in-depth, rich dialogue in order to make whole and vibrant the larger community of which we are a part. Successful community practices emerge from mutually agreed-upon guidelines for building trust. These may often include one person speaking at a time, refraining from dismissive statements, being fully present, speaking from one's own experience, respectful communication, paraphrasing to ensure accurate understanding of others' statements.

Authentic Listening: Habits of authentic listening serve as a bridge to excellent communication. Learn to concentrate on the intent of the speaker and the content of what is spoken. Tools include affirmation, nonjudgmental exchange, paraphrasing, and consistency between nonverbal cues and corresponding verbal messages. Of course, all such messages need to be culturally appropriate.

Conflict Resolution: Conflict resolution is a creative interchange leading to increased understanding and appreciation of each other. The interaction of different styles of conflict and conflict resolution is key. Learn different strategies for deflecting a conflict-driven situation in our houses of worship and in the larger world.

Communication: Practice skills to promote peaceable communication and collaboration. Learn how to identify communication roadblocks. Respecting differences, cooperation, making decisions, resolving conflicts, negotiation, and appreciating others all play a part in community building. Interpersonal relationships challenge us to use a wide range of skills.

Our Unitarian Universalist communities deserve the best of these practices.

Related Resources

Boers, Arthur Paul. *Never Call Them Jerks: Healthy Responses to Difficult Behavior.* Bethesda: Alban, 1999.

Fisher, Roger, and William Ury. *Getting to Yes: Negotiating Agreement Without Giving In.* New York: Penguin, 1981.

Goleman, Daniel. *Emotional Intelligence: Why It Can Matter More Than IQ.* New York: Bantam, 1995.

Leas, Speed B. *A Lay Person's Guide to Conflict Management.* Washington: Alban, 1979.

_____. *Leadership and Conflict.* Nashville: Abingdon, 1982.

_____. *Moving Your Church Through Conflict.* Washington: Alban, 1985.

McKay, Matthew, et al. *Messages: The Communication Skills Book*, 2nd ed. Oakland, CA: New Harbinger, 1995.

Palmer, Parker J. *The Promise of Paradox*. Notre Dame, Ind.: Ave Maria, 1980.

Peck, M. Scott. *A World Waiting to Be Born: Civility Rediscovered*. New York: Bantam, 1993.

Savage, John S. *Listening and Caring Skills in Ministry: A Guide for Pastors, Counselors, and Small Groups*. Nashville: Abingdon, 1996.

Schrock-Shenk, Carolyn, and Lawrence Ressler, Eds. *Making Peace with Conflict: Practical Skills for Conflict Transformation*. Scottsdale, PA: Herald, 1999.

Steinke, Peter L. *Healthy Congregations: A Systems Approach*. Bethesda: Alban, 1996.

Ury, William. *Getting Past No: Negotiating With Difficult People*. New York: Bantam, 1991.

Index

wounds from, 87, 147
See also specific religions
Religion Among the Unitarian Universalists, 111
Religions, 58, 130
Religious depth, 33
Religious education, 10, 39, 107, 126
    adult, 141
    and the Bible, 148
    classes, 126
    curricula, 148
    programs, 118
    Sunday, 101
Religious humanism, 23
Religious landscape of America, 40
Religious liberal, 55
Religious liberalism, 29
Religious liberals, 23
Religious naturalism, 73, 142
Religious pluralism, 140
Religious professionals, 141
Religious questions, 34
Report of the Committee on Goals (1967), 37, 115
Resolutions, 111, 115
Respect, 124
Retreat centers, 143
Reverence, 107
    See also Language of reverence
Richardson, Peter, 46, 47
Right relations, 82
Right relationship, 110
Risk-taking, 46
Rites of passage, 105
Ritual, 93, 125
Rituals, 40, 105
Robinson, David, 22
Romanticism, 73, 83
Roof, Wade Clark, 38
Roots, 72, 111
Ross, Warren, 127
Rumi, 82
Rush, Benjamin, 111
Russell, Bertrand, 82

Sacred, 74, 91
Sacred America, 112
Salvation, 3, 75, 89
    by character, 94
    universal, 21, 77
Santeria, 40
Santos-Lyons, Joseph, 122
Schulz, William, 67, 82
Science, 27, 85, 136, 142

Science and the Search for God, 78
Scovel, Carl, 77
Scripture, 17, 24, 67, 87
Seaburg, Carl, 102
Search committees, 82
Seder, 102
Segregation, 125
Self, 86, 118
Self-marginalization, 113
Self-naming, 71
Self-understanding, 47-48
Selling God, 40
Seminarians, 148
Seminary, 143
Sensory, 46
Sermon(s), 9, 99, 111
Service, 54, 55, 80
    elements, 98-100
    is prayer, 53, 103
Services, 138
Services (religious), 102
Seventh Principle Project, 111
Sewell, Marilyn, 80
Sexism, 115
Sexual morality, 111
Sexual orientation, 55
Shivvers, Charlotte, 91
Sikh, 40
Sin, 74-75, 89
Sinage, 118
Singing the Living Tradition, 99-100, 102, 103, 104, 105
Sinkford, William (Bill), 4, 6, 131
    and language of reverence, 4, 137, 140
    goals for UUA, 8
Skepticism, 47, 130
Skinner, Clarence, 127
Skinner, Donald, 113
Small group ministry, 13, 147, 150
Smith, Huston, 89, 90
Social action, 54, 111, 112, 131
    as ministry, 113
Social justice, 51, 72, 123, 146
Society (American civil), 39
Soul, 6
Soulful Sundown, 102, 118
Sources (UU), 70, 99, 106, 130
    non-Judeo-Christian, 88
    theological, 98
South America, 113
Southworth, Bruce, 37
Speck, Richard, 53-54
"Spirit of Life," 100-101, 105-106, 107
Spiritual depth, 143, 144

Spiritualities, 73
Spirituality, 6, 58, 72, 89
    and reason, 78
    cafeteria-style, 90
    embodied, 151
    "multilayered," 38
    personally defined, 36
    solo, 35
Spiritual journey, 2
Spiritual path, 90
Spiritual practices, 34, 143, 144, 145
Spiritual types, 47
Spoerl, Dorothy, 32
Stage theories, 49-51
Starhawk, 82
Starr King School for the Ministry, 4, 7, 14, 97, 145
    students, 9
Stewardship, 118
Stone, Jerome, 74
Stories, 70
Students (junior and senior high), 149
Study-Action Issues, 109
Supersessionism, 86
Survey, 101
Suzuki, David, 67
Sweet, Leonard, 86
Symbols, 88
Syncretism, 85

Taboo, 6, 151
Taoism, 73
Tapp, Robert, 111
Television, 31, 39, 40
Teshuvah, 110, 115
Thandeka, 76
Thanksgiving, 101-102
The Almost Church, 32
"The Changing Reputation of Human Nature," 76
The Communion Book, 102
The Free Church in a Changing World, 20, 23, 27, 140
The Humanist Pulpit, 55
Theism, 78, 84
Theists, 144
Theologians, 91
Theological fragmentation, 10
Theological identity groups, 9
Theological issues, 11
Theological language, 89
    See also Language of reverence
Theological legacy, 29